1

HOPE FOR CHALLENGED AIRLINE PILOTS
AN UNTOLD SUCCESS STORY

by

, **WARD B. BUCKINGHAM, M.D.**

ENDORSEMENTS

The author's father, Capt. Ward Buckingham, was one of the early pioneers who dared enter the dangerous societal waters dealing with airline pilots and alcoholism. Prior to the 1970's, any licensed airline pilot who was deemed alcoholic received a lifetime permanent banishment from ever flying again. As the result of the combined efforts of those early pilot pioneers, medical doctors, and the FAA, the HIMS program was born in 1973. Over 6,500 recovering alcoholic pilots have been returned to the cockpits. It is perhaps the single-most successful recovery program ever put in place.

Captain Lyle Prouse, retired airline pilot and author of Final Approach

Captain Ward Buckingham was saddled with the potentially devastating disease of alcoholism at a time when the disease was misunderstood and often ridiculed. In an industry whose attitude was typically to deny that a problem existed or to summarily fire the affected pilot, he, with help from his family and friends and colleagues, was not only able to confront and control his illness. He was also a groundbreaking leader in helping airlines acknowledge and address this disease among their pilots, support rather than ignore or humiliate or fire those who fell victim to it and establish one of the most effective programs in any major industry today. With this book, we now have a comprehensive look back at the progress made by our airline industry from the darker ages of naivety and denial to today's more truly 'Golden Era' of aviation where pilots who need help can readily and effectively receive it. Sit back, relax, and enjoy this journey!

Jack G. Modell, M.D. Vice President and Senior Medical Officer, Rho, Inc.; author of "Drinking and Flying: the problem of alcohol use by pilots." NEJM 1990

With this frank story of his father's years of addiction and eventual redemption, author Ward Buckingham gives us an inside look at what was once a taboo subject in the airline industry. The reader will worry, wonder and then cheer as this intrepid airman makes the long journey from impairment to becoming a spokesman and champion for recovering alcoholics.

Robert Gandt, former Pan Am captain and best-selling author of Skygods: The Fall of Pan Am and more than a dozen books of aviation and military history

This book describes the dogged persistence required by the author's father to help bring about a vitally important change in US aviation law regarding the handling of pilots addicted to alcohol: now known as the HIMS program. This story provides valuable insight on how recovery programs can be designed and implemented to benefit other safety-critical industries and encourage and support family members of addicted relatives. It also reminds us that even the very best proposals for change can take a long time to implement and gain acceptance.

Capt. Peter Wolfe, executive director Professional Aviation Board of Certification (PABC)

The HIMS program has saved many lives and careers over the years. The success of this program is a model for demonstrating how the airlines, unions and Federal government (FAA) can work closely together for a common good. Dr. Buckingham has truly captured one pilot's story while providing us with a historical perspective of the process. Thanks to him for recognizing the many persons involved with the program's creation and development over the years, individuals (many no longer with us) to whom much is owed.

W. Keith Martin, M.D., M.P.H., Aviation Medicine Advisory Service (AMAS) chairman

This book puts a human face on a turning point in the destigmatization (removal of the association of shame or disgrace) of alcoholism and recovering alcoholics. Ward (the author's father), and other courageous pilots who came forward, significantly helped the effort allowing recovered commercial pilots to return to productivity as airline pilots.

Barton Pakull, M.D., FAA Chief Psychiatrist in Office of Aviation Medicine (1971-2003)

ACKNOWLEDGEMENT

I am indebted to Niki Anderson for editing my manuscript. Her remarkable ability to be concise whereas I tend toward the verbose, her corrective application of American grammar, since I was educated in British grammar, and her attention to detail all have been key in creating this finished product. I feel most fortunate to have benefitted from this multi-published author who taught writing courses at Spokane Community College and at many writers' conferences in the Pacific Northwest.

Thanks also are due Lyle Prouse for his thoughtful and constructively critical comments over the months of this writing project.

Finally, thanks are due to my father without whose story I would never have been moved to write this book. Not one of us is perfect, and he demonstrated that adversity can indeed lead us to higher ground if we recognize reality and respond positively. Granted, he needed coercion by threat of job loss, but from that came a willing servant dedicated for his remaining lifetime to helping others trapped in the bondage of addiction he himself had experienced.

CONTENTS

DEDICATION

You may be tired of the legions of written works, "when bad things happen to good people." Perhaps your life story thus far has been uniquely fortunate and devoid of such tribulation. Sometimes, though, we gain helpful insight through the eyes of others as they recount their personal life challenges. It is with that goal in mind that I share this story. In doing so, I want to dedicate this prose to two family members: our dear mother and my talented middle brother, Mark.

Mother dutifully stood with my diseased father long enough to see great good come out of a lengthy season of suffering. While unwittingly serving as the classic, and classy, enabler, Mother's behavior and that of fellow airline employees (and other family members including yours truly) doubtless delayed Dad's recovery from addiction. However, his subsequent role as a recovered alcoholic airman, supported by Mother's insights gained on the journey, leaves a legacy of good from which all can benefit.

Mark's desire to fly like Dad was actively discouraged by Dad during the worst phase of his alcoholism. One could reasonably argue that Dad's negative view of the future of airline pilot life was distorted by his ongoing deep immersion in booze as his solace. As a result, Mark garnered a college degree in education and taught for several years before Dad (now recovered from alcoholism) agreed to send Mark to United Air Lines flight school in Denver to help train for his second career as an airline pilot. Sometimes timing is everything, and Mark was competing for jobs with qualified Vietnam trained pilots exiting the military. As a result, Mark had to join a small airline initially while his high school classmate was already a senior pilot with a major airline before Mark even landed his first pilot job. Brother Mark therefore bore the brunt of the negative effects of our Dad's addiction amongst us three boys in my judgment, but I never heard him complain.

During the recovery phase, my parents weathered yet another monumental disaster when my youngest brother, former Washington State Patrol trooper Mike Buckingham, survived a drunk driver-caused fiery career-ending crash with seven months burn center recovery. *Triumph Born of Ashes* was my first book and was dedicated to Mike's two children.

INTRODUCTION

Imagine yourself a passenger on Pan Am's London to Los Angeles Boeing 747 in early 1970's with actress Elizabeth Taylor seated on the captain's lap steering that one-million-pound bird as it jockeyed for position at its assigned arrival gate in LA. Or better yet, how about being a passenger on Pan Am's Boeing 707 leaving Seattle with the captain so drunk he had to be helped up the stairway by two fellow crew members and strapped in the cockpit's jump seat well removed from aircraft controls! But as far as passengers and airline management and FAA regulators knew, the captain remained in command of that flight on paper and over the PA system so that the 'secret' reality of his impaired state never left that cockpit and crew. Yep, both examples are absolutely true, and they illustrate a time in aviation history I label the 'dark ages' which others choose to call the 'golden age' of flight. My father was that captain in each case.

Let me be clear: this book is not intended to disparage the character of pilots, the competence of government regulators, or the courage of airline management. After all, who can fairly criticize those who are ignorant of a reality and hence impotent to effect change in that reality. Denial of reality is a different matter. Knowing reality, but denying its existence, is fair game for lodging criticism. This book will expose how pilots, regulators and airline management dealt with impaired airmen in what I'll label 'the dark ages,' before the 1970's. My father's life will be used throughout. In the end the reader will be encouraged to learn that achieved progress benefits all three participant categories and, most importantly, the safety of the traveling public. For overseas foreign airlines many are just now beginning to act in the arena of impaired airmen that the U.S. began over 40 years ago (personal communication, Lyle Prouse 2/1/2017). Alcoholism is no respecter of persons. It afflicts men and women, young and old, employed and unemployed, white collar professionals and common laborers, rich and poor, famous and unknowns. The only people spared the risk of becoming alcoholics are those who choose to never drink alcoholic beverages.

No full-length book exists which tells what you are about to read. Yes, numerous news articles have appeared for public consumption over the 100+ years of aviation. An example is a Chicago Tribune August 30, 2016 article titled "Intoxicated in the air: Drunk pilots make news but are rare." Trade journals and newsletters and government regulators' white papers exist and will be cited throughout this account. The bottom line is we humans are imperfect regardless of chosen vocation. But for some lines of endeavor the consequence of committing error can be life-changing. That is certainly true in my world as a physician, now retired and speaking and writing about enhancing patient healthcare safety. It is glaringly real when contemplating the fate of a heavier-than-air tube containing up to several hundred humans operated by pilots in whom we place our trust for safe flight.

My goal is for readers to get a grasp on the reality of the pre-HIMS (Human Intervention Motivation Study) era of hidden/enabled pilot alcohol dependency and the process by which that changed throughout the 1970's to lead to greater airline safety and employee pilot health. I want to again emphasize that my intent is *not* to disparage or demean the character of pilots. In fact, it was a core of pilots who persevered in the 1970's to effect that needed change in how alcohol dependency was viewed by management, pilot union and government regulator factions. Alcohol dependency is so common in our society that virtually every adult reader knows of someone in their sphere of influence with the disease, alcoholism. Some of you know of pilots who are still flying while in bondage consequent to current alcoholism. Please do not ignore your opportunity to bring deliverance to that friend, co-worker or loved one by being the loving enabler that my dear mother was to my father for so many years. The diseased one will only be farther down the dead-end road of terminal alcoholism allowed by your inaction. I hope, then, to be a catalyst for readers' activism in moving present practicing closet alcoholic airmen to treatment and rehabilitation. Why? Because human nature still leads some to deny and/or hide their alcohol dependency. The HIMS program manager of one large airline has told me the following: "Many of our pilots are doing well in their recovery. Unfortunately, there are many many more that would benefit from this program but are not ready to do so."

You will find some relevant contact information in my chapter nine and appendix I with names, phone numbers and websites which can help you help those pilots in need of help with their alcohol dependency. "The only thing necessary for the triumph of evil is for good men to do nothing." Think about that and do your part for the good of humanity around you. When it comes to confronting the alcoholic mired in denial, you do well to enlist the helping guidance of recovered alcoholics. Nobody knows the practicing alcoholic's con game like one who has been there and is now solidly recovered and rehabilitated. No one can wish their way out without the help of others who have been there and understand the reality of their predicament. While the current FAA surgeon general is correct stating (personal communication) "the public will be of limited value in motivating airline pilots to seek help through the HIMS process," a significant minority who were prompted by friends and/or family have achieved lasting sobriety and relicensing through the HIMS process.

In no way do I wish to diminish the personal responsibility of those who choose to drink and drive or drink and fly. But I believe we all must come to grips with the reality that alcoholism is a disease, not simply viewed as a moral failing or sign of personal character flaw. Alcoholics are sick and in bondage to their addicted lifestyle. As such, we all need to be on the alert for this disease and we must guard against assuming the "enabler" role which serves only to prolong the suffering of all involved and the increased public safety risk posed by those choosing to drink and operate either aircraft or land-based vehicles. Knowledge is power, but it must be applied in real life lest it remain simply knowledge for knowledge's sake. Use the helps identified in this book.

Let my tale begin. As a prelude I give you a tantalizing view of reality as it existed prior to what I'll label the transformative 1970's, and these are the words of Dr. Richard Masters, arguably the most important person in facilitating this transformation in approach to alcohol dependent airline airmen:

> In the early 1970's, no system-wide method of helping airline pilots with alcohol problems or alcoholism had evolved. Some commercial air carriers had recognized the need for occupational alcoholism programs; but few, if any, professional pilots had availed themselves of the meager early programs. The public image problems faced by the pilot's union, the air carriers and the Federal Aviation Administration (FAA) served as a powerful damper to keep the cases hidden. There was a wonderfully synergistic relationship between alcoholism, the supreme manifestation of which is denial, and the fears of pilots, companies and government regulatory agencies manifesting themselves as denial that such problems existed. Hence, the alcoholic pilot denied he had a problem; his fellow pilots, fearing they could cost him his career, denied he had a problem; his supervisors reacted similarly; and the company simply announced they had no alcoholics on their property. The FAA could 'prove' there was no problem, since they almost never got an application from a pilot who proclaimed he was an alcoholic (and if they did, they would efficiently deny certification permanently). So, this mini-society of commercial aviation continued for many years in a conspiracy of silence and denial, unwilling and unable to own the truth that alcoholism was a disease that no more spared pilots than any other segment of society.

CHAPTER ONE
IN THE BEGINNING

My father was born in the lumber town of Kalispell, Montana in 1918. His father, a lumberman, settled there in the 1890's. Dad's birth followed his siblings by 12, 15 and 17 years making him the baby of the family. His mother died as a result of a grievous medical error in 1929. Her only functioning kidney was surgically removed in Portland, Oregon, in what has commonly now been referred to as "wrong-sided surgery," and that was three decades before dialysis was available.

Dad's first airplane ride was at age 13 in 1931 with legendary Alaska bush pilot, Robert Campbell "Bob" Reeve, at the controls of a Boeing 80A trimotor. That experience fueled his goal of flying and his future career as a pilot. His first recollection of alcohol ingestion was as a child during a family feast of Welsh rarebits, typically cheese melted with ale or beer and served over toast. That was the start of associating alcohol with fun. A handwritten outline for an address to the National Council on Alcoholism in 1977 includes the entry, "prescription during prohibition." That, and the heavy-drinking neighbor whose friend had a still both suggest he journeyed into drinking as a teenager.

Once he was old enough to drive, he worked summers driving logging trucks. Logging crews often took their Friday paychecks and spent their earnings on heavy drinking over the weekend. Presumably, Dad participated in some of that activity during his summers of logging.

As an older teen he wanted a motorcycle, but his dad did not approve. They reached a compromise. His dad would send him to Great Falls, Montana for two summers where he would live with his sister and brother-in-law while taking flying lessons. And so, he began his flying career with lessons from Palmer-Spring Flying Inc. in Great Falls.

Although both his father and older brother were lumbermen, Dad chose to attend college and major in engineering. At the University of Montana in Missoula, he excelled academically. He also spent increasing amounts of free time at "Jocko's gym," the nickname given to the bar in Missoula's old Park Hotel.

Johnson Flying Service had begun training pilots in 1926. Dad taught flying lessons there during his college years approximately 1937-1941 which helped pay for college. It was a well-known flight school for training smoke jumpers. Although he attempted to join the Air Corps and Navy, he learned from a friend that Pan American World Airways (PAA) was hiring pilots for their Alaska division which prompted my parents to relocate to Seattle where he was hired as a "junior pilot" on February 18, 1942.

Of note is the fact that Bob Johnson's Missoula Flying Service trained more than 4,000 pilots in 1942 for the US armed forces. Dad was promoted to "master pilot," commonly known as "captain," in 1945. He had spent most of WWII flying troop supply missions to the Aleutian Islands as PAA had contracted with our US government in support of the war effort. Although he himself never flew the Clipper flying boats, they were still being used by PAA during the war and often carried VIP's.

For example, President Franklin Roosevelt secretly travelled to and from the Casablanca summit meeting with Churchill, Stalin and De Gaulle in January 1943 aboard PAA's Boeing-314 (named Dixie Clipper). At FDR's 61st birthday celebration on January 30, the only participant not to take a sip of champagne was the flying boat's Captain Howard M. Cone because aviation regulations did not permit the pilot to drink while on duty.

I need to point out a feature of airline pilots' flight assignments, especially international carriers like PAA and particularly in the pre-jet era of air travel. Flight crews consisted of captain, co-pilot, engineer, navigator and stewardesses. Many overseas flight plans involved layovers of several days before making the return flight to home base. It was not unusual for flight crews to party in the local bars and night clubs at such outposts. Although I know of no disciplinary action against Dad in his 36-year career with PAA, he himself told of others who got soused, raised a ruckus and got beat up as a result. One especially colorful happening was in Beirut, Lebanon.

Base transfers were part of life for PAA pilots, and Dad had the choice of moving to Beirut or London England in early 1950. Fortunately, he chose London where an American salary allowed for comfortable living.

The folks rented a six-acre estate in Wentworth 20 minutes from Heathrow, London's main airport. Our home, Westwood, adjoined the 11th fairway of the East Course of famed Wentworth Golf Club. It was owned by a young master at exclusive Eton who also owned a Jaguar dealership besides the Westwood property.

David lived in a separate cottage adjacent to our large home. The underground bomb shelter, which was used throughout WWII, had been converted to a wine cellar. Unexploded ordinance was still being found in our neighborhood during our 1950-1955 life there.

A large formal dining room on the main level was the site of numerous raucous parties during those years, and the large silver punch bowl we now have saw heavy use of alcoholic drinks then. Amazingly, I'm not aware of Dad ever getting a DUI anytime in his adult life although once, when in a drunken state, he wrapped a beautiful green 1952 MG roadster around a tree when we lived there.

One of the happiest days of my life was in August 1955 when the folks informed us boys that we'd soon move back to the U.S. I was age 12 and had lived away from home eight months each of the three previous years while attending boarding school. Life there was spartan, food terrible and discipline extraordinary. C.S.Lewis' book, *Surprised by Joy*, includes a vivid portrayal of boarding school life like mine although his experience preceded mine by three decades.

I was 'allowed' to visit home one Sunday each month from 10AM to 4PM. Homesick boys who ran away from school were flogged in their parent's presence on return to the school. Why did my parents send me there, you ask? They were told by other Americans based there that boarding school education was far superior to government school education, and that was undoubtedly true.

I studied Latin and French for three years each, Greek for one year and algebra and geometry. However, I was socially backward, and that experience certainly didn't do anything to foster familial closeness. The cultural experience living in close contact with 100 other boys ages 6-12 hailing from 35 different countries of our world was indeed unique.

Meanwhile Dad's flight schedule usually involved two lengthy trips a month to East Asia with layovers sometimes stretching over a week. The folks seemed to be happy, but I imagine drinking was an increasingly important part of his layovers. As far as we know he had not yet started to hide bottles of booze at home. His job performance remained extraordinarily high by all accounts. Indeed, I have a letter sent Aug. 4, 1955, by Mr. S.D. Bechtel (then President of San Francisco-based Bechtel Corporation) to his friend Juan Trippe (then President of PAA) which reads in part:

> Knowing of your interest in the special services given by your organization, I wanted to drop you this note. July 28th, I rode on your PAA Flight #1, Beirut to London. The ship was under the direction of Captain Buckingham. It was one of the best flights of the many hundreds that I have taken. Captain Buckingham not only handled the plane splendidly but also handled the crew and the passengers, both in the air and on the ground, with courtesy, thoughtfulness, and effectiveness. The ship was clean when it left Beirut and still clean when it arrived in London some 15 hours later. Captain Buckingham is one of the most outstanding aviation officers I have ever seen, and I wanted to send on this note and call it to your attention.

PAA management chose to forward the letter to Dad and make it part of his personnel file.

Our family moved back to Seattle in late 1955 by way of Hong Kong, Tokyo and Honolulu, enjoying fascinating and memorable several day stays at each location. Dad continued to build on his outstanding reputation with PAA and was tapped twice for several months each time 1958-1960 to serve as acting Chief Pilot for the Pan-Alaska region.

I was in high school then and was working out of town during summers, hence not around home to observe Dad when he was off duty. He was responsible for my 'in' getting that summer job at a lake resort in NW Washington state. The owners were nice folks but drank rum and Cokes continuously every evening. Wayne had a seaplane and each week would ferry one of us three male employees up to the satellite operation 20 miles away. He was a former WWII bomber pilot and an incredibly hard worker.

One trip is especially memorable. He and I were in the plane together with several 5-gallon cans of gasoline which I would sell to fishermen at the satellite float. The takeoff was typically east from the dam toward the log-boom above the dam. He overestimated his ability to get adequate lift before hitting the log boom. As we approached at increasing speed, he realized he was not going to break free from the lake surface and proceeded to do a 2-pontoon right drift to pass successfully through the narrow gap in the boom. I wonder what his BAC (blood alcohol concentration) was? It had been approximately 10 hours since his last flotilla of rum and Cokes!

I recall a story shared by Dad about a fishing trip there with one of his men's groups. They would stay several nights in the rustic accommodations at that floating resort and join the owners' drinking soirees. One of my Dad's pilot cronies boasted about tripping on the log walkways while carrying an alcoholic drink one night, falling full length across the water between two adjoining log walkways and managing not to spill his drink. Such were the drinking escapades of this crowd when not flying.

CHAPTER TWO
BOOZE TAKES OVER

The story moved forward in the 1960's. Hiding bottles of hard liquor became typical for Dad though many were not discovered until many years after 1966, the year he achieved lasting sobriety. My middle brother, Mark, recalls times when Dad was staggering drunk at friends' parties a few miles from our home. Yet he would successfully drive Mother home with the two younger boys (I was away at college) and himself. Sometimes Mother was successful in getting into the driver's seat before him. He was never abusive or violent when drunk; just simply a sorry-appearing shell of his normal sober self.

Mark recalls that he was often the one from 1961-1963 in his high school years to pick up Dad at Sea-Tac on arrival home from a flight. The State liquor store was on the seven-mile route to our house, and Dad seldom failed to insist on stopping there to buy more booze. While he was still in his flight uniform, he was always careful to remove his identity badge, epaulets, captain hat and captain suit jacket before entering the store. Wise move since a member of the nationally-famous 1990 Northwest Airlines arrested crew made himself and his pilot job loudly known to patrons in a bar where they were drinking, and an appropriately concerned patron blew the whistle on them!

Looking at Dad's condition for work, he was sometimes not as careful. In fact, on more than one occasion Mark drove him to Sea-Tac for flight duty and enablers abounded all around. While Dad was the captain of record for the flight, he never touched the controls but rather sat strapped in the cockpit jump-seat sobering up.

Flight check-in was accessed on the north end of the Sea-Tac airport complex, entering underground via a one-way roadway to pull up at lower level curb. Two uniformed crew members would then emerge from the side-door by Operations and unload Dad from our car. They proceeded, one to each shoulder, shepherding him through doors (by-passing flight crew check-in) and out to the front stairway entering the Boeing 707 to which they were assigned. Yes. This really happened. More than once!

Dad knew he had a problem, but denial is an oft used defense mechanism. Can I point to any increased stress in his life that might have played a role in driving him to drink more? I do note that Dad's 3-ring binder of important papers related to his Pan Am career is devoid of entries after the February 11, 1960, letter of appreciation from management for his "outstanding job as Acting Sector Chief Pilot" until his extended medical grounding of January 14, 1966, except for two notable items. One is a copy of the letter Professor C. G. Jung in Zurich wrote on January 30, 1961, replying to Mr. William G. Wilson, the Bill W. co-founder of Alcoholics Anonymous in New

York. How Dad came upon these letters is unknown to me, but their placement in this binder tells me the content of the letters were of great import to him. Furthermore, their location tells me he acquired them prior to the second item's filing which suggests that he had enough interest in A.A either to research on his own or be directed to these resources. Bill W's letter of January 23, 1961 reads as follows:

My dear Dr. Jung:

This letter of great appreciation has been very long overdue.

May I first introduce myself as Bill Wilson, a co-founder of the society of Alcoholics Anonymous. Though you have surely heard of us, I doubt if you are aware that a certain conversation you once had with one of your patients, a Mr. Roland Hazard, back in the early 1930's, did play a critical role in the founding of our fellowship.

Though Roland Hazard has long since passed away, the recollections of his remarkable experience while under treatment by you has definitely become part of A.A. history. Our remembrance of Roland Hazard's statements about his experience with you is as follows:

Having exhausted other means of recovery from his alcoholism, it was about 1931 that he became your patient. I believe he remained under your care for perhaps a year. His admiration for you was boundless, and he left you with a feeling of much confidence.

To his great consternation, he soon relapsed into intoxication. Certain that you were his "court of last resort", he again returned to your care. Then followed the conversation between you that was to become the first link in the chain of events that led to the founding of Alcoholics Anonymous.

My recollection of his account of that conversation is this: First of all, you frankly told him of his hopelessness, so far as any further medical or psychiatric treatment might be concerned. This candid and humble statement of yours was beyond doubt the first foundation stone upon which our society has since been built.

Coming from you, one he so trusted and admired, the impact upon him was immense.

When he then asked you if there was any other hope, you told him that there might be, provided that he could become the subject of a spiritual or religious experience---in short, a genuine conversion. You pointed out how such an experience, if brought about, might re-motivate him when nothing else could. But you did caution, though, that while such experiences had sometimes brought recovery to alcoholics, they were, nevertheless, comparatively rare. You recommended that he place himself in a religious atmosphere and hope for the best. This I believe was the substance of your advice.

Shortly thereafter, Mr. Hazard joined the Oxford Groups, an evangelical movement then at the height of its success in Europe, and one with which you are doubtless familiar. You will remember their large emphasis upon the principles of self-survey, confession, restitution and the giving of oneself in service to others. They strongly stressed meditation and prayer. In these surroundings, Roland Hazard did find a conversion experience that released him for the time being from his compulsion to drink.

Returning to New York, he became very active with the "O. G." here, then led by an Episcopal clergyman, Dr. Samuel Shoemaker. Dr. Shoemaker had been one of the founders of that movement, and his was a powerful personality that carried immense sincerity and conviction.

At this time (1932-34) the Oxford Groups had already sobered a number of alcoholics, and Roland, feeling that he could especially identify with these sufferers, addressed himself to the help of still others. One of these chanced to be an old schoolmate of mine named Edwin Thacher. He had been threatened with commitment to an institution, but Mr. Hazard. and another ex-alcoholic "O. G." member procured his parole and helped to bring about his sobriety.

Meanwhile, I had run the course of alcoholism and was threatened with commitment myself. Fortunately, I had fallen under the care of a physician—a Dr. William D. Silkworth---who was wonderfully capable of understanding alcoholics. But just as you had given up on Roland Hazard, so had he given me up. It was his theory that alcoholism had two components---an obsession that compelled the sufferer to drink against his will and interest, and some sort of metabolism difficulty which he then called an allergy. The alcoholic's compulsion guaranteed that the alcoholic's drinking would go on, and the allergy made sure that the sufferer would finally deteriorate, go insane, or die. Though I had been one of the few he had thought it possible to help, he was finally obliged to tell me of my hopelessness; I, too, would have to be locked up.

To me, this was a shattering blow. Just as Roland Hazard had been made ready for his conversion experience by you, so had my wonderful friend, Dr. Silkworth, prepared me.

Hearing of my plight, my friend Edwin Thacher came to see me at my home where I was drinking. By then, it was November 1934. I had long marked my friend Edwin for a hopeless case. Yet here he was in a very evident state of "release" which could by no means be accounted for by his mere association for a very short time with the Oxford Groups. Yet this obvious state of release, as distinguished from the usual depression, was tremendously convincing. Because he was a kindred sufferer, he could unquestionably communicate with me at great depth. I knew at once I must find an experience like his or die.

Again I returned to Dr. Silkworth's care where I could be once more sobered and so gain a clearer view of my friend's experience of release, and of Roland Hazard's approach to him.

Clear once more of alcohol, I found myself terribly depressed. This seemed to be caused by my inability to gain the slightest faith. Edwin Thacher again visited me and repeated the simple Oxford Groups formulas. Soon after he left me I became even more depressed. In utter despair I cried out, "If there be a God, will He show Himself". There immediately came to me an illumination of enormous impact and dimension, something which I have since tried to describe in the book, "Alcoholics Anonymous", and also in "A.A. Comes of Age", basic texts which I am sending you.

My release from the alcohol obsession was immediate. At once I knew I was a free man.

Shortly following my experience, my friend Edwin came to the hospital, bringing me a copy of William James' "Varieties of Religious Experience." This book gave me the realization that most conversion experiences, whatever their variety, do have a common denominator of ego collapse at depth. The individual faces an impossible dilemma. In my case the dilemma had been created by my compulsive drinking and the deep feeling of hopelessness had been vastly deepened by my doctor. It was deepened still more by my alcoholic friend when he acquainted me with your verdict of hopelessness respecting Roland Hazard.

In the wake of my spiritual experience there came a vision of a society of alcoholics, each identifying with, and transmitting his experience to the next---chain style. If each sufferer were to carry the news of the scientific hopelessness of alcoholism to each new prospect, he might be able to lay every newcomer wide open to a transforming spiritual experience. This concept proved to be the foundation of such success as Alcoholics Anonymous has since achieved. This has made conversion experiences---nearly every variety reported by James---available on an almost wholesale basis. Our sustained recoveries over the last quarter century number about 300,000. In America and through the world there are today 8,000 A. A. groups.

So to you, to Dr. Shoemaker of the Oxford Groups, to William James, and to my own physician Dr. Silkworth, we of A. A. owe this tremendous benefaction. As you will now clearly see, this astonishing chain of events actually started long ago in your consulting room and it was directly founded upon your own humility and deep perception.

Very many thoughtful A. A.'s are students of your writings. Because of your conviction that man is something more than intellect, emotion and two dollars' worth of chemicals, you have especially endeared yourself to us.

How our society grew, developed its traditions for unity and structured its functioning, will be seen in the texts and pamphlet material that I am sending you.

You will also be interested to learn that in addition to the "Spiritual experience", many A. A.'s report a great variety of psychic phenomena, the cumulative weight of which is very considerable. Other numbers have---following their recovery in A. A. ---been much helped by your practitioners. A few have been intrigued by the "I Ching" and your remarkable introduction to that work.

Please be certain that your place in the affection, and in the history of our Fellowship, is like no others.

Gratefully yours,

William G. Wilson

Co-founder Alcoholics Anonymous

Dr. Jung's reply, dated 30 January 1961 which was only five months before his death, offers profound spiritual insight:

Dear Mr. Wilson:

Your letter has been very welcome indeed.

I had no news from Roland H. anymore and often wondered what has been his fate. Our conversation which he has adequately reported to you had an aspect of which he did not know. The reason that I could not tell him everything was that those days I had to be exceedingly careful of what I said. I had found out that I was misunderstood in every possible way. Thus I was very careful when I talked to Roland H. But what I really thought about was the result of many experiences with men of his kind.

His craving for alcohol was the equivalent on a low level of the spiritual thirst of our being for wholeness, expressed in medieval language: the union with God (ref.).

How could one formulate such an insight in a language that is not misunderstood in our days?

The only right and legitimate way to such an experience is that it happens to you in reality and it can only happen to you when you walk on a path which leads you to higher understanding. You might be led to that goal by an act of grace or through a personal and honest contact with friends, or through a higher education of the mind beyond the confines of mere rationalism. I see from your letter that Roland H. has chosen the second way, which was, under the circumstances, obviously the best one.

I am strongly convinced that the evil principle prevailing in this world leads the unrecognized spiritual need into perdition if it is not counteracted either by a religious insight or by the protective wall of human community. An ordinary man, not protected by an action from above and isolated in society, cannot resist the power of evil which is called very aptly the Devil. But the use of such words arouse so many mistakes that one can only keep aloof from them as much as possible.

These are the reasons why I could not give a full and sufficient explanation to Roland H., but I am risking it with you because I conclude from your very decent and honest letter that you have acquired a point of view above the misleading platitudes one usually hears about alcoholism.

You see, Alcohol in Latin is "spiritus" and you use the same word for the highest religious experience as well as for the most depraving poison. The helpful formula therefore is: <u>spiritus contra spiritum.</u>

Thanking you again for your kind letter I remain yours sincerely

Ref: 'As the heart panteth after the water brooks, so panteth
my soul after thee, O God' (Psalm 42:1)

It is now clear to me why Dad repeatedly credited A. A. and faith in a higher power for freeing him from the bondage of a boozed-up life. But I believe that Dad needed his equivalent of the Edwin T. that Bill W. finally had to achieve lasting sobriety, and that came later (January 12, 1966) in the form of Jim N., the "personal and honest contact with friends" mechanism that Jung says is one of three ways for the alcoholic to achieve a "higher understanding." The absence of that mechanism earlier and the reality that the 10-day Schick aversion therapy approach of July 1964 failed must have combined to create increasing stress of perceived hopelessness portrayed so vividly in Bill W.'s letter. Add to that the likelihood that Dad's supervisor probably gave verbal warnings over some time period to Dad regarding his drinking before formalizing same as a letter of ultimatum (which follows shortly).

The second item of likely stress in this six-year early 1960's period, which is otherwise devoid of documents, relates to some possible cardiac issues and their impact on his medical recertification. Dad received a mailing dated March 4, 1964, from the FAA regional Flight Surgeon expressing concern over an EKG which had been done November 29, 1963, at his regular exam. The three-month lag points out a major weakness of government processing which hopefully is not typical of today's FAA efficiency in monitoring pilot health in the interest of preserving the safety of the traveling public.

That letter stated: "It is routine procedure for all ECG tracings for Class One applicants to be sent to our research center in Georgetown for study. After review of your ECG, their interpretation indicated a slight abnormality." Specific instruction then followed about options for him to satisfy FAA requirements, one of which was to get a cardiac consult either with the Los Angeles FAA examining facility or his own locally.

Dad chose the local option and his internist provided what was requested which apparently reassured the FAA sufficiently to grant him the medical certificate renewal. In retrospect, my own medical practice experience tells me that numerous variations from normal can be seen in ECG's of practicing alcoholics, and this time period was deep within Dad's worst drinking years.

His later survival in 1982, despite medical malpractice that would have shuttered the life of many 64-year-olds, is testimony to his healthy heart status. However, that month of uncertainty over whether he would be grounded for cardiac reasons was stressful as would be the threat of health issues ending any airline pilot's livelihood. The tone of Dad's initial reply to the FAA's March 4 letter further tells me he was unhappy with their request and hence stressed over it.

Mother told us that Dad went through Schick Shadel's alcoholism treatment program at least twice and failed to achieve lasting sobriety. I was in contact with Schick in 2017 and they could only confirm his patient status as active for 7/15/64-7/24/64. Nevertheless, their aversion therapy program did not work and that was what I witnessed as typical during my experience in internal medicine practice.

Aversion therapy programs have a higher post-treatment relapse rate than standard 28-day in-patient treatment programs followed by A.A. maintenance. Those aversion therapy programs are based on the premise that punishing the drinking of alcohol will extinguish the drinking behavior, and the punishment can either be inducing emesis using Antabuse or delivering electric shocks triggered by the ingestion of alcohol. Although I do not favor aversion therapy and have a basis for my bias, I need to acknowledge the reality that what works for one person might not for another. Schick claims to cure 70 % of those who complete their aversion therapy-based program.

In September 1965 during my first year of medical school in Seattle, Mother called one day asking to meet with me. My strong submissive mom had reached the end of her rope. She had packed her bags and told my youngest brother Mike, age 12, that they were leaving Dad. And what did young Michael say to that? "I'm not leaving Dad!" So, she shared the dilemma with me. We talked for two hours seated near the medical school complex, and she chose not to leave Dad.

But somewhere in the final months of 1965, Dad had attended an A.A. meeting sponsored by recovering alcoholic Jim N. I do not know how many meetings they attended in those months, but it was enough to develop some sort of bond.

Between the A.A. meetings, his out-of-control drinking and hiding of bottles continued to grow. A January 6, 1966 mailing from Dad's chief pilot, the one he had subbed for in 1958-1960, was probably received on or about January 9. It was the ultimatum Dad desperately needed to read:

Dear Buck:

This letter will formally advise you in regard to your status with Pan American. Your accrued sick leave was fully liquidated as of Dec. 15, 1965. At that time you were placed on vacation to liquidate all earned vacation which will terminate effective January 14, 1966. Therefore, beginning January 15, 1966, you will be off the payroll.

It is our sincere desire that you should return to active flight duty at the earliest possible time; however, from all the professional and expert advice we have received it is too soon to return at this time. Several months are required to fully rehabilitate one's self, so I suggest we take a look at the situation on April 1, 1966 and decide whether or not more time is required.

It is our plan to place you on an indefinite Medical Leave of Absence effective January 15, 1966. During this leave you must adjust yourself physically and psychologically to total abstinence from alcohol which is the prime requirement before you can return to flight duty. When you do present yourself for reinstatement you should be prepared to provide adequate evidence that you have your problem under positive control.

We wish you well and anytime we can be helpful please feel free to give us a call.

Best regards, Sector Chief Pilot-SEA

For a man accustomed to be the one in control this call to action was new and devastating. His very livelihood was now at once on the line. Jim N. confirmed that Dad's last drink was January 12, 1966. Jim, himself a recovered alcoholic, responded to Dad's call regarding the job ultimatum. He picked Dad up and the two of them checked into a motel near the Sea-Tac airport where Jim kept Dad confined and away from alcohol for several days while Dad proceeded to sober up. Jim then rode herd on him to assure he got to A.A. meetings several times a week initially. January 13 of 1966 was Dad's first day of permanent sobriety! He was so thankful to Jim that he provided financial backing for Jim's shoe repair business to expand, initially into a commercial building Dad owned and later into the Bon Marche stores throughout the Sea-Tac region. Some years later Dad and his business partner decided to gift all those shoe repair business locations and equipment to Jim. Dad's and his business partner's futures were financially secure, but Jim had only social security to sustain his retirement. Jim's role in assuring Dad's A.A. attendance was certainly key to saving Dad's livelihood and life.

Despite Dad's illness, alcoholism, his character was positive in his drinking days among those around him. I know of few living pilots who were fellow crew members of his in those days. Nick recalls meeting Dad when brother Mark was racing quarter-midget race cars in 1956 as an 11-year-old. Nick was fresh out of the military, and Dad encouraged him to take flying lessons. He followed through and got on with Pan Am. I pressed him about whether he had any awareness of Dad's alcohol abuse and he could come up only with one vague recollection when he was a second officer on a Honolulu to Seattle flight of Dad's. Nick did not view Dad as fitting the typical "sky god" image of the arrogant or domineering captain. Instead he remembers him as a great model. For example, he recalls a landing that he (Nick) made at Hilo in windy weather, and the landing was not one of Nick's best. He felt down on himself and it showed. Dad encouraged him rather than making critical or demeaning remarks.

Bob was a member of Dad's flight crew many times in the early 1960's including several flights where he could tell Dad had been drinking. Hap recalls one morning event when Dad was obviously impaired as he reported for flight duty. Dad, apparently noting Hap's observation about Dad's condition, said "Jack is going to be doing a lot of flying today." Dad was referring to his co-pilot assigned to that day's flight.

CHAPTER THREE
COCKPIT DISCIPLINE & COMMAND PILOT STRESS

Imagine for one moment that you were a passenger on board an early 1960's Pan Am flight departing from Sea-Tac. Your cabin attendant team leader comes on the cabin microphone with the usual welcome announcement to passengers: "Welcome aboard Pan Am flight 801 to Honolulu. Your Boeing 707 is piloted today by Captain Ward Buckingham assisted by first officer Charlie-the-Enabler."

Then recall my brother Mark's experiences driving Dad to Sea-Tac where he was manually assisted by fellow crew members up the stairs into the cockpit and securely strapped to the jump seat well removed from the plane's controls. How do you suppose Dad's fellow crew members felt about their incapacitated leader and boss, and their actions in lying to the passengers who were trusting their safety to the named flight crew? Complicit were the smiling cabin attendants aware that the team leader was in fact out of action, and the rest of the ten or so flight crew team who knew they too were party to the deception of the company's management and the airline industry's safety and competency regulator, the Federal Aviation Administration?

Do you suppose that Dad's inebriated presence in that cockpit might have posed a bit of a distraction for his colleagues seated nearby? So much for cockpit discipline! Mind you, I'm forever thankful to that team of enablers for not blowing the whistle on Dad for the simple selfish reason that his career and our family's livelihood (and very tangible assistance with financing my college education ongoing at the time) was dependent on Dad's airline wages. Of course, I'm even more thankful that his impaired state was recognized by his peers who acted to protect the safety of their passengers and themselves by sidelining Dad. Cockpit discipline and the matter of flight crew alcohol abuse are intimately related.

Dad shared a story late in life of a vivid illustration of breech in cockpit discipline of nearly lethal consequences. During our early 1950's stay in England, he was captain of a Pan Am crew dead-heading a Lockheed Constellation returning to London from the Far East. Aboard that return trip, there were no passengers...only the flight crew. While I have no knowledge whether alcohol or drugs played a role in the crew's behavior, the story still illustrates how crucial discipline is in the airplane cockpit.

Dad was tired and decided to go back into the cabin to nap, leaving the other three flight crew in the cockpit to fly the aircraft. That was common on such lengthy flights. However, for some reason known only to the good Lord, Dad awoke earlier than he planned. Looking out the cabin window, something about what he saw just did not look right. He returned to the cockpit and asked those flight crew members where the plane was relative to their original flight plan. None of the three could immediately answer his question. Cruising along at that airplane's usual altitude top of about 22,000 feet, it turned out they were approximately 200 miles north of their intended course. Had they continued inattentively along and had darkness enveloped them, they would likely have impacted one of numerous Himalayan peaks along their altered course of flight. They had become thoroughly distracted by some cockpit activity rather than piloting the plane. Lesson learned! Cockpit discipline is vital. In fact, Pan Am's vice-president of flight operations, himself a senior pilot, circulated a September 16, 1971, memo focused on highlighting the crucial import of cockpit discipline:

> Since 1967 we have experienced five accidents in the descent/landing phase of flight. To refresh your memories, accidents occurred at Berlin, Montserrat, Caracas, Calcutta and Manila. All resulted in fatalities. That is a rate of about 1.1 per year. An extraordinarily high rate! It is extraordinary also because, to the best of our knowledge, there were no mechanical problems involved and if weather was a factor, it was a minor one. Why then did these accidents occur?

> The official 'probable causes' are now matters of record except for Manila. Probable causes are derived from examining the facts available after each particular accident. Over the past few weeks I have been examining our collective record for the past five-year period. From this examination it appears that regardless of the probable cause of these accidents, there is a basic similarity in all of them. The conclusion is subjective but if you could read the records and listen to tapes I am sure you would reach the same conclusion.

> The thread which underlies all of these accidents is discipline, or rather the lack of discipline. I'm not referring to punitive discipline or punishment, but rather the discipline of conduct; the kind of discipline that Webster describes as a "rule or system of rules affecting conduct or action," or "to develop by instruction and exercise, to train in self-control or obedience to given standards."

> In each of these accidents there seems to have been failure of discipline characterized by an apparent failure to validate information essential to flight safety. As captains, you have the obligation to always demonstrate and to insist on adherence to discipline. In the cockpit, you and your crew must perform all duties in accordance with the procedures in which you were all trained.

One of the basic requirements in the exercise of command is to have a plan. A good commander makes his plan known to his crew. A well-disciplined crew speaks out when things aren't going according to plan. A well-disciplined crew reviews the whole plan when essential parts of the plan require change.

The operating procedures in the aircraft manual, if followed, should have prevented the five cases cited above. Apparently, for some reason the procedures apparently were not fully applied. Some people would call this complacency. I don't! I call it discipline. Self-discipline: the discipline necessary to refuse shortcuts, the discipline to speak out when things aren't moving in accordance with the plan, and the discipline to abandon a plan in the face of altered circumstances and establish a new plan. From what I have been able to learn from the information available from the five flights involved, these disciplines were not present.

I hope you will dwell upon the aspects of this conclusion rather than debating its merit. Because whether I'm right or wrong, a good deal of serious thought on how you fit into this subject will stand us in good stead. You and your crews in particular. The subject of this letter is so sensitive and important that I have used this unusual method of communication...addressed only to Captains. While it is expected to generate and it should generate discussion and thought within the airline, it would be appreciated if it were handled as "Very Confidential."

The above captain-only mailing *did* indeed generate discussion. One response from a senior PAA captain read in part:

...the time is long past that the pilots are going to accept the Random House definition of discipline ('a whip or scourge, used in the practice of mortification, or as an instrument of chastisement...') which you actually practice, rather than the Webster's definition to which you pay lip service, but really have never applied. In conclusion, I am debating the merits of your system and you are dead wrong. A great deal of serious thought is going into how to cope with such an unprecedented mid-management attack on selected employees by another employee.

This irate captain cited several examples of fellow pilots where the captain felt the management mailer had made unfair discipline decisions, basically viewing management as increasingly heavy-handed in how they dealt with captains. His vigorous response was by no means the only one that raised a fuss over the tenor of this confidential mailing. Did this and other irate captains' responses simply reflect guilty consciences threatened by exposure of their true shortcomings? Did any of these responders have alcohol abuse or alcoholism problems so far hidden from management? Did any of those five fatal Pan Am accidents to which the first writer referred involve alcohol-impaired flight crew errors or omissions? We will never know the answers to those important questions.

I digress for a bit to point out that the airline industry, recognizing especially in the 1970's the need to understand the reasons for increasing accidents in order to prevent them, pioneered its seemingly obsessive compulsive present approach to safety which the medical field is only recently borrowing from to transform from a culture of self-protectionism or concealment to a culture of safety and transparency.

A simpler label for transparency and safety is honesty with the traveling public; honesty provided willingly by the airline, and without prodding from the legal community. For example, every cockpit crew should have a check list for preparation for takeoff and a checklist for preparation for landing. There should be no distracting influences on the pilot crew at these key times as they perform their job.

An illustration of undesirable distraction (from safety standpoint) is provided by Dad's letter to Pan Am Flight Standards Committee chairman March 30, 1972 in which he stated:

> It has come to my attention that new hires are being told in their transition training program to use the interphone system for their 'cabin secure report.' The <u>attention</u> required by operating crew <u>during engine start should not be diverted</u> by answering cabin interphone or listening to the chime thereof. The subject report should be given in person by the hire or designee.

The four-engine 747 of which he was speaking, the aircraft he was then commanding, is a very complex machine demanding carefully synchronized team cohesion for safe efficient operation. Similarly, the operating suites of hospitals now expect surgical teams to have 'time-outs' when the entire team of nurses, doctors, therapists and assistants in a very mechanical compulsive way determine that the right patient is prepped on the operating table for the right operation on the correct side of the body with known allergies clearly understood by all. Typically, whether in the airplane cockpit or the operating room, any present team member is empowered with both the right and the responsibility to speak up promptly if they see or hear anything that is out of line. That work environment atmosphere has been referred to variously as "situational awareness," "cockpit resource management," or "culture of safety."

Lest you think Dad and other "Skygods" (Robert Gandt's title for his 1995 book about the fall of Pan Am) were all business in the cockpits of their 'castles in the air,' they made room for occasional levity. Case in point is a returning trip via the polar route from London to Los Angeles, probably in the early 1970's. As he approached

LA, the cabin crew informed him that a VIP, the actress Elizabeth Taylor, was on board. Dad instructed them to invite her to the cockpit while he called the control tower at LA to request a special favor. Would they sing a 'welcome home Liz' ditty when he gave the cue? They readily agreed and Ms. Taylor entered the cockpit and was seated in the jump seat behind Dad for the landing. After touchdown, head phones were supplied to Ms. Taylor who then enjoyed the live 'welcome home Liz' greeting from the tower. Realizing it would be several minutes on the ground before they could dock at their assigned gate, Dad turned around and asked her if she would like to drive the plane while they taxied toward their assigned arrival gate. Receiving an enthusiastic answer in the affirmative, he then invited her to sit on his lap to steer the big plane which she did. Would this occur today? Not a chance, especially since 9/11, but even before that event, FAA and company regulations had been tightened and air marshals were added unannounced to some flights.

While system failures seem more common and profoundly impacting on safety results both in medicine and aviation, individuals are not excluded from potentially bearing primary responsibility for safety failures. Let me illustrate with an experience from my own medical practice. I preface my remarks by emphasizing that my patient was not harmed by what I did or did not do.

She was a very pleasant 85-year-old active lady with aortic valve heart disease. Four weeks earlier her diseased native valve had been replaced with an implanted mechanical valve which required life-long anticoagulant therapy to prevent that valve from getting gummed up and plugged, a lethal result incompatible with life. The fluid accumulation in the previously opened chest cavity had failed to resolve, and that necessitated needle drainage (thoracentesis) of that left-sided pleural effusion. I had performed hundreds of these procedures over the years.

The sterile instrument utilized includes a large-bore metal needle for puncturing the skin into the chest cavity whereupon a smaller gauge plastic catheter is advanced until 'locked' in place against the hub of the needle. The metal needle is then withdrawn from the chest cavity leaving only the plastic catheter inside same. Either a large syringe with three-way stopcock or vacuum bottles with same are attached to the plastic catheter and the chest fluid is then drained until dry or until patient symptoms require stopping the procedure. For reasons entirely obscure to me, I began the fluid drainage part of the procedure with the metal needle still inside her chest cavity until after approximately 100 cc of the anticipated 1000 cc had been drained.

Suddenly it dawned on me that I had failed to follow precise procedure performed hundreds of times previously over my career. Remember I am performing this procedure with my patient therapeutically anticoagulated. It is therefore even more important that I not initiate bleeding. This large bore metal needle is now 2-3 inches inside her chest cavity directly behind her heart which is, of course, moving with each beat.

Suppose that the needle inside her chest had rubbed against the sac (pericardium) surrounding her heart. Or worse, suppose the needle had punctured her pericardium and heart muscle and entered a chamber of her moving heart. I recall vividly breaking a major sweat as I realized my error, corrected same and proceeded to complete the procedure without any trouble or later need for further thoracenteses.

To this day I have no explanation or excuse for my break in proper procedure. But I speak and write regionally to both consumer and provider audiences about enhancing patient healthcare safety and advocacy. An abbreviated reference to this illustration of my personal but unintentional medical errors is part of that PowerPoint presentation.

Returning to Dad and flight safety, it is well known that stress contributes to disease including alcoholism. Piloting aircraft, particularly large aircraft like the Boeing 747 which can carry up to 600 passengers depending on configuration, is demanding, even stressful. Stress itself is not all bad. It depends on how we respond to the perceived stressors.

The event I'm going to share now occurred six years into Dad's sobriety on March 20, 1972, as captain of Pan Am flight 002, a Boeing 747 destined for Tokyo. Following is Dad's written account sent to Pan Am regional Flight Standards Committee chairman in Los Angeles:

> Severe frontal activity and single runway operation required holding at Oshima and Onjuku for approximately 90 minutes. Approach clearance was received for ILS [instrument landing system...author added] to 33R with circle to land 15L. Continuous monitoring of Tokyo weather indicated ceilings 1000 to 1200 feet, visibility 7 to 9 km winds 21'0 to 26'0... gusts 20 to 40. I requested runway 22 but was told it was closed for noise abatement (an outright lie). Oh yes, rain was falling.
>
> The circling approach was made with proper air speed adjustments added for gusts. Touchdown was made in a smooth wing-low no drift manner about 1500 to 2000 feet from approach end. Speed brakes, differential reverse and wheel brakes applied at once. TRAP: as stated in aircraft operating manual 'keep directional control by use of flight controls'. POINT: how to hold steady brake pressure when using rudder and aileron to counteract gusts. The memory system in anti-skid must be modified. Had the runway been 1000 feet shorter, the machine would not have

stopped on the runway. I will not attempt an approach under similar conditions again.

The reason for the closure of runway 22 was not, as I had been told, for noise abatement. Runway 22 is closed at 2100 nitely so airplanes can be <u>parked</u> thereon!! This sad state of affairs led to the following fiasco:

(1) The next airplane to land after us suffered a knocked-off nose wheel, closing the entire airport for about 7 hours

(2) The closure prevented our flight 002 from departing for Honolulu

(3) The crew assigned for the onward 002 cancelled after 5 hours and went back to hotel

(4) Capt. _____ and crew assigned then to take delayed 002 to HNL–LAX removing them from Delhi pattern

(5) Remaining San Francisco-based Capts. _____ and _____ had allowed their Hong Kong qualification to expire necessitating Buckingham and crew taking Capt. _____'s Delhi pattern. Extra cost to Pan Am due crew disruption alone estimated $5,000

To prevent a recurrence of the above I recommend the following:

(1) Convince Tokyo airport authority not to park aircraft on runway 22 during periods of strong southwesterly winds. Runway 33L can be used for parking during these times

(2) Provide some penalty for crews who do not maintain qualifications over routes to which they may be assigned

(3) Provide projector and appropriate airport films at Tokyo to prevent repetition of above crew foul-up

(4) Revise 747 brake system anti-skid circuitry to prevent complete brake loss with changing pedal pressure.

Dad had been a 747 captain for 15 months and a Pan Am pilot for 30 years when this occurred. He was well known and respected within the flight crew ranks and management for his safety-conscious written reports like this throughout his career.

An earlier and scarier event illustrates that as long as human beings are the actors on the stage of real life, errors will happen. This near-disaster occurred either just before or just after he achieved permanent sobriety in January 1966. Rest assured Sea-Tac is a safer facility than it was that foggy day. Dad was the captain of a Pan Am 707 jet flight destined for Portland, Oregon, and then on to Honolulu. The records are conveniently unavailable now. No planes were allowed to land in the dense fog, but takeoffs were permitted. As the jet reached V1, the point of no return past which there is no safe aborting of takeoff, he saw a green blur out of his left field of vision. At ground speed he was traveling approximately 200 feet per second. Instantaneously, he concluded the green blur was an object traveling toward his aircraft in line with the port two engine pods. His fellow crew members were each interviewed days later by my brother, Mark, who was years later also to become a jet pilot. They reported to him that they had never seen done, in all their combined aviation careers, what Dad did next. He abruptly pulled back on the stick and "hopped" the full-size sedan driving down the runway. He continued on to takeoff speed and an otherwise uneventful trip. The elderly couple in the sedan were uninjured but understandably frightened, the trunk of their vehicle having been blown open and up into the roof by the jet engines' exhaust blasts. A small utility gate toward the northeast end of the airport had inexplicably been left open, and these folks were simply lost in the fog. Had the aircraft been carrying a full load of passengers and fuel, Dad might well have been unable to clear that object. He had a penchant for writing when cause célèbre presented itself, and this incident generated huge reactions from all directions among those concerned with safety of the traveling public and flight crews.

Further stress plagued pilots with the ever-present threat of job and career loss due to unfavorable FAA decisions about pilot fitness to be licensed. Unlike college professors, commercial pilots do not have tenure though they do have a strong and active union, the Air Line Pilots Association (now named Air Line Pilots Association, International) or ALPA. It is not surprising that he bristled at government edicts threatening pilot job security. This June 1972 letter addresses what appears to be a questioning of airline medical examiner honesty by P. V. Siegel, the FAA Federal Air Surgeon at that time. It is unclear to whom Dad sent this missile. The content follows:

> Re: FAA's Federal Air Surgeon, P.V.Siegel
> How long will the medical community tolerate the above-mentioned individual's accusations of dishonesty and/or incompetence? His original accusations were directed at his own

agency's appointees. He has now accused the airline-employed medical examiners of dishonesty in the performance of their very valuable service to the public in the practice of industrial medicine. The 'union safeguards' mentioned by Siegel are properly provided to protect the pilot in the event of a faulty diagnosis threatening his career and are brought into action only when the pilot's personal medical practitioner does not agree with the original diagnosis. A third 'disinterested' medical officer then renders an opinion and whichever of the two previous diagnoses he confirms becomes binding. Enclosed you will find a copy of a 'typical' pilot agreement page describing this procedure.

Siegel's professed concern would be valid if the records showed a scheduled passenger fatality due to physical incapacitation of the flight crew. Granted, men have died at the controls of aircraft and have become otherwise incapacitated. This is one reason why we have more than one man at the controls of the airliner you ride as a passenger. Men will continue to die at the controls or become otherwise incapacitated regardless of the type of physical exams given and regardless of the identity of the examining official and the comprehensiveness of his examination.

Siegel should address himself to the real physical and mental health safety problems involved in the operation of high-performance jet aircraft through eight or nine time zones into marginally-equipped airports with marginal weather conditions. Another interesting study would involve the physiological effects of continuous exposure to abnormally high ozone levels ambient at high flight levels.

As an average airline pilot, in the past twelve typical months I have:

1. Spent over 900 command hours aloft in 747 aircraft

2. Had two thorough physical examinations given by an FAA designated medical examiner with an extensive aviation medical background

3. Had an equally thorough medical examination given by the company Medical Department

4. Thrice demonstrated my proficiency to company check pilots accompanied by FAA personnel in a simulator

5. Once demonstrated my proficiency to a company check pilot accompanied by FAA personnel in 747 aircraft (items 4 and 5 are known in industry vernacular as 'six months proficiency checks' and are performed generally six hours in the simulator and two hours in the aircraft at the controls)

6. Twice over an eight-hour stage length flight demonstrated my capability to safely accomplish the mission to company check pilots

May I pose the following questions: who checks Siegel's mental and physical condition and who certifies his competence and how much recurrent training does he accomplish?

My father was not shy as you have no doubt gleaned from text thus far. Dad now sober and cured? Right? He never took another alcoholic drink in his remaining 28 years of life. But the label, alcoholic, never left him. A reminder of that reality appeared the next year. Another Pan Am captain had been terminated in 1967, and a factor in common with Dad's history was alcohol abuse. ALPA (the pilots' union) had been negotiating unsuccessfully with the company for the captain's reinstatement. The ALPA lawyer had filed a grievance protesting the captain's termination, and Dad was provided a copy of that grievance document by his ALPA council chairman since Dad was named in it. Key parts of the grievance document follow:

...with regard to my preparation of his case I feel it would be useful if I had all the facts surrounding the Company's decision to retain _____ _____ and Ward Buckingham in its employment after they allegedly committed certain acts of gross misconduct. My understanding is that this misconduct was highly offensive to the Company and definitely detrimental to its operation, but in spite of these obvious grounds for termination the Company decided not to discharge them. I think the situation of these two pilots and the attitude the Company adopted with respect to their right to retain their jobs would be pertinent to the propriety of Captain _____'s termination. Therefore, I would appreciate it if you could furnish me as soon as possible with the following information: 1) the type of employment records these two pilots had prior to their misconduct, 2) the dates and nature of their misconduct, 3) any mitigating circumstances which tended to explain or justify the misconduct, 4) the type of disciplinary or remedial action taken by the Company with respect to each of these pilots after the misconduct occurred. *(Note: I have intentionally omitted names from this and following quotes to protect identities.)*

The Chairman of the ALPA Council for Dad's region wrote him this regarding that lawyer's request:

> Dear Ward:
>
> Enclosed is the letter I spoke to you about the other evening in San Francisco. Since then I have discussed the case with our Standards Committee Chairman...and we investigated ALPA policy manual. We do not feel...that the case in question is at all similar to yours...will write ALPA attorney something to that effect; however, we leave it entirely up to you whether you comply with his request or not.
>
> Ward, it is only because I know you as well as I do and respect you for what you have done that I find it possible to even forward this letter and this request and I beg of you not to take offense, as none is certainly intended from anyone.

Dad's reply was immediate:

> Re: your letter of 2 June 1967 and that of ......12 May 1967. 1) I have not been apprised of the circumstances regarding the case of Captain _____, 2) as far as I know no charges of 'gross misconduct' were made by the Company in my 'case,' 3) I committed no acts of 'gross misconduct' while on Company property or while on duty, 4) I would suggest that the defense of Captain _____ be made on the premise that he was or is ill under the strictest of medical definitions, 5) if you feel that an investigation of my 'employment record' would be of help in this case, this letter constitutes my permission for your review of such record in my presence if the Company concurs, 6) I have nothing to hide.

As it turns out, this adventure did not end there. A year later Dad penned the following, obviously provoked by some behind-the-back shenanigans that give cause to men like him who have beaten the disease of alcoholism but are still dogged by its stigma.

Gentlemen of the MEC: 13 May 1968

How the ALPA legal department obtained the hearsay information regarding my 'certain acts of gross misconduct' is of no real importance. However, I must object to an apparent attempt to go behind the scenes in the attempt to gain information concerning an individual without first obtaining his concurrence.

In cases such as the subject terminated pilot, ALPA and the MEC would be well advised to tread with caution before they become prostituted by their defense of a pilot against whom the Company holds all the cards. Experience has demonstrated, on other lines besides our own, that when a pilot calls for ALPA assistance in this matter, the case has already progressed too far.

Those of us who have fallen into the trap of alcoholism are certainly not blameless. My previous misdeeds cannot be erased however much I would will it so. Complete atonement for my actions is impossible of accomplishment, but I stand ready and willing to help any individual who wants assistance before his actions make the case irreversible.

You who have never been faced with this ever-growing malady are incapable of understanding the insidiousness of it. You ask 'why doesn't he just lay off the booze, can't he see what he's doing to himself?'

Gentlemen, it is not quite that simple, but time does not permit me to bore you with the description of a terrifying, hopeless, helpless, living hell on earth.

Should you ever have knowledge of anyone who is affected by this disease, and who wants assistance, my phone is available and I'll go anywhere at any time to help.

I'll leave this thought with you. Any man who is engaged in this profession and who uses alcohol is exposed to the disease; it is not deferential of personalities.

The last of the twelve steps central to Alcoholic Anonymous reads: "Having had a spiritual awakening as the result of these Steps, *we tried to carry this message to alcoholics* (emphasis added by me), and to practice these principles in all our affairs."

And that is exactly what Dad was conveying when he said that he would go anywhere at any time to help. I was away immersed in the rigors of medical school, but my brothers confirmed that anytime they were visiting our folks, the phone would be ringing off the hook regarding some airman somewhere with some airline who needed help for alcohol abuse problems. As a physician myself, I can attest to the fact that one of the best things an individual recovering from alcoholism can do to strengthen the permanence of his sobriety is to reach out and help others trapped in the bondage of booze.

The April 1967 issue of Seattle, the Pacific Northwest magazine of that era, featured a five-page article written by noted area author Emmett Watson who accompanied Dad on one of his Honolulu trips which included FAA-authorized seating in the cockpit jump seat. Watson noted at an initial get-acquainted lunch that Dad refused alcoholic beverages offered, and he attributed Dad's refusal "to a natural wariness in front of a reporter scheduled to discuss airline pilots..." Dad later explained it this way: "I quit it two years ago when I discovered that social drinking was a bore." Hogwash! But remember 1967 was still 10 years before Dad felt comfortable about 'coming out' with a public 'confession' that he was a recovering alcoholic. It was still six years before the FAA would grant the very first exemption to a pilot with alcoholism history and allow him to retain the licenses required to pilot aircraft. Dad still had a potential 11 years as command pilot before reaching the mandatory retirement age of 60 years.

As Lyle Prouse rightly observed in reviewing my manuscript: "No one is 'cured' from alcoholism. I'm an alcoholic for life because the disease is only arrested, not cured. I may be a 'recovering' alcoholic but an alcoholic nonetheless. It's alcohol-ism, not alcohol-wasm."

CHAPTER 4
ALPA & AN ALCOHOLIC'S ACTIVISM

The ALPA, label for Air Line Pilot Association, was founded in 1931 eleven years before Dad was hired as a commercial airline pilot. ALPA is the world's largest pilot union, and, from its inception, their mission has been "Schedule with Safety." Each member airline has its representative leadership which interfaces with the national leadership of ALPA. Typically, each airline then has a Master Executive Council (MEC) representing/leading multiple (number depending on pilot geographic dispersal and number) local executive councils (LEC).

Two years into Dad's new-found permanent sobriety in 1968, he informed Pan Am MEC of his alcoholism history and recovery as well as his passion and availability for helping other similarly diseased airmen to recover. About this same time, ALPA opened their first Aero Medical office, and in 1973 he was appointed as PAA MEC Aeromedical Coordinator. Meanwhile Dad had made initial contact with Dr. Richard L. Masters, ALPA's first Aeromedical advisor tapped for that position in 1969.

The two men collaborated closely for the next several years while concerned activism hit a feverish pitch on the matter of alcohol-impaired flight crew. In 1972, Dr. Masters made his first presentation on the previously hush-hush matter of pilot alcoholism at ALPA's Board of Directors. While former airline captains Rod Gilstrap (UAL) and Gil Chase (Continental/UAL) are acknowledged as the main ALPA airmen credited with contributing to Dr. Masters' successful application of the HIMS (Human Intervention Motivation Study) program, Dad was an important contributor also. Indeed, Dr. Masters penned a letter April 29, 1977 supporting Dad's application to the FAA for an exemption for alcoholism medical recertification. He stated in part:

> I have known Ward since 1972 and have worked closely with him many times in conjunction with his duties as Aeromedical Coordinating Committee Chairman, PAA. Additionally, I have had opportunities to work with him on a personal basis when he has participated in training seminars for ALPA aeromedical coordinators and, later, in the formative work leading to the development of the ALPA HIMS program. Ward has been an invaluable advisor to me and the HIMS staff and I consider him to be most knowledgeable in the area of alcoholism. Virtually single-handedly, Ward has spear-headed the formalization and maturation of a working alcohol rehabilitation program on his own airline and his leadership has gained the respect of all concerned. Perhaps an even more important activity has been his work in developing Birds of a Feather Alcoholics Anonymous programs in several metropolitan areas of the country. The 'Birds' groups are well-known to provide superlative recovery-strengthening

programs, allowing pilots to relate to peers in working through their specialized problems. Hence, Ward has been a tireless worker for PAA pilots as well as his brother airline pilots.

Of interest is the fact that Dad's written notice to the Chairman of PAA MEC and the LEC Chairmen, dated October 23, 1973, recommended each LEC appoint an aeromedical coordinator, and he informed them of Dr. Masters' availability as a resource for achieving "return to active flying" for pilots who had FAA medical certification problems. Dad also had a copy of his letter sent to Captain R. W. Gilstrap. A letter sent March 19, 1974 to Dr. Masters by Dad epitomizes the working relationship of these two individuals on behalf of their fellow man:

Dear Dr. Masters:

As a result of our phone conversation regarding your assistance to the troubled pilot in Minnesota, in which case I understand the FAA has become involved, I make the following observations. These observations are based on my own experience and that of those with whom I have worked. I realize my opinions may be at variance with the disciplines of psychiatry and, at times, medicine.

A definite period of abstinence before returning to duty after medical treatment for alcohol abuse or alcoholism is a must. This for the individual's benefit as well as for those who are concerned with his sobriety. Proper medical treatment in an institution oriented specifically toward the treatment of alcoholism does return the individual to a state of relatively good physical health if he has not progressed too far down the road. Psychiatric treatment during the medical therapy probably helps.

When the individual is discharged from the treatment center, he is usually thrust back into the same environment that produced the problem in the first place. Unless he personally sought the treatment through his own volition, there seems to be little likelihood of attaining permanent sobriety without the individual's associating himself with Alcoholics Anonymous. I don't mean to infer that medical and psychiatric therapy are not helpful. However, the individual must change his mental outlook on life and his opinion of himself if he is to achieve happy sobriety. If he doesn't attain happy sobriety, he won't be sober very long. 'Total permanent abstinence' are the three most abhorrent words to the practicing alcoholic and, without the help and understanding of those who have experienced his affliction, he is (in his opinion) the most frightened lonely frustrated and unlucky individual that ever lived. His confidence and ego are shattered and, for a pilot, a big share of each is required. Browbeating by a panel of psychiatrists does not help.

As I mentioned, a minimum of ninety days abstinence seems to be indicative of the individual's dedication to sobriety providing he has associated himself with A.A. and his sponsor is willing to attest to his determination.

I was most happy to hear of your success in obtaining the grant and hope to be of assistance.

Sincerely,

Ward Buckingham

cc: Rod Gilstrap

I need to digress briefly to acknowledge another important man in Dad's life---a senior captain with United Air Lines (UAL). Both had common backgrounds as recovered alcoholic airline pilots, and he was the subject of widely published news reports in 1976 as a result of saying on national TV before the Washington Press Corps, "I'm an alcoholic."

UAL quietly started working in 1968 to develop assistance for employees whose work was suffering because of drinking problems. In 1971, the program was formalized by the UAL Board of Directors and announced in an industry publication by then UAL President Eddie Carlson. This took foresight and a lot of grit on the part of Mr. Carlson. He set an irreversible trend in the industry. Dad's UAL friend himself had achieved lasting sobriety two years before Dad. I believe they met as a result of their individual efforts with their respective airline's ALPA trailblazing on behalf of alcohol-impaired airmen. They shared speaker roles at several national and regional meetings in the 1970's, and Dad's friend was the founder of the Burlingame, California, Birds of a Feather nest a year after Dad co-founded the initial Pacific Northwest nest. They remained closest of friends until Dad's death. His heart-felt comments to my mother on January 3, 1995 read in part:

Dear, dear Dodie,

I share the grief with you in the loss of my old and dear friend. The parson above must have decided that he had won all the prizes here, and that it was time to call him home. The legacy that Captain Ward Buckingham left for airmen will be honored and nurtured by those he left behind for years to come; particularly so for those of us in the world-wide nests of "Birds" that are his creation. I wanted to be with you for the memorial service but my doctor has a tight rein on me for now. My love to you and the boys.

(signature omitted to preserve anonymity consistent with A.A. practice)

Reflecting over such historical documents, it becomes apparent that these men---Dr. Masters, Rod, Dad, Dad's UAL friend and many others---were blazing a trail hitherto untraveled. Collectively, they realized the importance of teamwork, the open sharing of ideas and knowledge. We of the air-traveling public are all benefactors of those historical efforts, especially as it relates to air travel safety. But stop to consider another reality: nearly all of us have been, are or will be touched in some way by the alcohol problems of a relative, friend or co-worker. Humans helping fellow humans should be a universal part of the character of each one of us.

Three months later June 28, 1974, Dad penned a ground-breaking letter to PAA's Vice President of Operations, Dan Chandler, which reads as follows:

> Many thanks to you for arranging the meeting with Dr. Constantino. The subject problem is of such serious nature as to cut across all generally accepted management-association lines. I personally congratulate you and Dr. Constantino on your enlightened approach and acceptance of our mutual responsibility in this area. The keystone to our solution, I believe, lies in the recruitment of a sufficient number of recovered alcoholic airmen. Somehow, they must be assured of immunity in order to smoke them out of the woodwork and volunteer to participate in this field. Generally speaking, experience indicates recovered alcoholics are anxious to help if they can identify themselves to management with impunity. The prime reason for this is the instinct of self-preservation. The recovered alcoholic must never forget how bad it was and working with those still suffering reinforces his sobriety.

> Compassionate as they may be, 'earth people' (i.e. those who have not experienced this affliction) cannot fully understand the ego and soul-shattering terror resulting from the realization by the airman that he has a problem he cannot solve alone. After all, has he not survived these many years through his knowledge and skill? Hopefully, the presence of a recovered brother airman during the confrontation phase will elicit an admission when the affected individual sees living proof of the existence of help and hope.

> I believe any success we may have must follow along these tentative lines: 1) recognition of the existence of the problem, 2) confronting and convincing the individual that he has an alcohol-related problem, 3) treatment and reorientation at a specified facility, 4) surveillance after the accomplishment of the three steps indicated. Phase 1 should not be too difficult an accomplishment without resorting to 'spy' techniques. Medical director's diagnosis,

physical appearance, discreet inquiry from crew members, the close association of check airmen, reference to performance profiles, consultation with instructors, airman's chronic use of sick bank time, airman's chronic late reporting, all provide clues.

Phase 2 should be accomplished in the presence of the Base Director of Flight Operations (Chief Pilot), Senior Base or Area Medical Director, Chairman of the LEC, and recovered airman. The troubled airman should be confronted with evidence as available and must be assured of the company's and union's desire to help, not censure. The recovered airman should then briefly outline his background so that the troubled one will realize at least one of the group has been there and back.

If admission of the problem's existence is forthcoming, the individual should agree to attend a recommended facility while either being paid a 'retainer' at a subsistence level while on administrative leave or using 'sick bank' time on minimum guarantee. Treatment costs should be borne by the individual or insurance used if alcoholism is not specifically excepted from the coverage.

Should an admission not be forthcoming, but evidence is overwhelming in the diagnosis of alcoholism, the airman should be either medically or administratively grounded and forced to accept treatment at a specified facility as a requirement for continued employment. Pay and treatment costs as in 2 (a) above. Many avenues of coercion are available and must be discussed at length.

Phase 3 treatment and reorientation should be taken at a facility following the whole person and A. A. approach as used at Alcenas. The period of required grounding probably will vary with the individual and whether or not the FAA has become involved. It has been demonstrated that successful treatment will produce an employee better able to perform his function than the pre-problem employee unless irreversible physical or mental damage has been done. Requalification costs will be minimal. I recommend the ALCENAS treatment approach and strongly urge that anyone who may have a part in our endeavor study THE EMERGENT COMPREHENSIVE CONCEPT OF ALCOHOLISM by James R. Milam, ACA Press, PO Box 266, Kirkland WA 98033, and become fully conversant with the concepts set forth therein. Studies of publications on alcoholism available from NIAAA U.S. Dept. of H.E.W. are also recommended.

Phase 4 (surveillance after return to active service) should not be a problem. Discreet inquiry from co-workers provides the best source and if the individual has fallen once, he'll be doubly watched on his return—especially by junior. Should the individual decide on 'some post-graduate work', experience shows that his deterioration is dramatic (i.e. his pattern starts where it stopped when he accepted treatment---uncontrolled).

How many chances does the individual get? What chances are given the diabetic?

Copies of this were also sent to Dr. Constantino, Dr. Masters, PAA Medical Director, PAA-MEC Chairman. It should be noted that Dr. Joseph G. Constantino was Corporate Medical Director of Pan Am. Mr. Chandler unfortunately met an untimely death the next year at age 42, and I wonder if loss of that high ranking management ally in Dad's mission to effect change in how corporate viewed and dealt with alcoholic airmen hindered the whole process, contributing to Dad's later letter of frustration of 1976 soon to be cited.

Dad's leadership presence in ALPA as MEC Aeromedical Coordinator served as an important catalyst for the following mailing to all PAA flight crew members under the signatures of Chairman PAA MEC and Vice President PAA Flight Operations dated July 10, 1974. That PAA MEC chairman was a longtime friend of Dad and our family, and his son has given me permission to use his Dad's name, Captain Lyman (Mike) Watt:

Note to All Flight Crew Members

The subject of health maintenance is of paramount importance to all airmen. No other line of endeavor has, as a requirement for continued service, the successful completion of three physical examinations per year.

Studies tend to indicate that a⁻ major cause for early termination of airline careers is alcohol abuse and its associated pathologies. A moment's contemplation is in order here while you consider known cases of medical or early retirement or death listed as myocardial infarction, hepatitis or other liver malfunction, neurological disorders, etc. when the root cause was alcohol.

In most cases no favor is being done an airman suffering from alcoholism who is allowed medical retirement under the guise of some other physical disability. He won't live long enough to deplete the retirement fund to any great extent and the life he does live will be most unpleasant.

Nationwide studies indicate that at least 10% of the general population is alcoholic and that perhaps another 15% suffer in varying degrees from the results of alcohol abuse. There is no reason to believe that a cross section study of a group of airmen, if it were made, would vary essentially from the nationwide figures. Recovery from alcoholism is successful in degrees from 0% to 80% depending on facilities used and individual motivation.

A number of airline companies sponsor successful alcoholism recovery programs open to all personnel, but with little airman participation due to the popular misconception that airmen, being supermen, do not develop alcohol problems, and if they do, they are terminated for moral or physical reasons and left to continue their unhappy way of oblivion. The reluctance of an airman to identify himself with other airmen alcoholics is understandable due to licensing requirements and his fear of reprisal if the 'awful' truth becomes known publicly. He also hesitates to admit, even to himself, what he has been led to believe is a weakness but is in fact an illness.

There is no indication that alcohol abuse has been a factor in any way in incidents or accidents involving Pan American aircraft. However, the Company and Pan American MEC desire to establish the first alcoholism recovery program in the industry specifically oriented toward the airman. This enlightened step comes from our recognition and new understanding that scientific rationale is available now as never before and more knowledge is gained almost daily. Low-cost model treatment programs are available to individuals, recognizing that this illness requires treatment and should not be written off as stemming from character defects or moral degeneracy. More of the technical background will be supplied as the program advances, but in the meantime we jointly view this as a significant milestone in the airline industry: the first honest recognition that airmen are not exempt from the pertinent statistics, as well as an honest desire to put available recovery programs to work rather than relegate our affected airmen to obscurity.

There are many ways you may take part in this program. If you have had experience of any kind in this area, be it through A.A., ALANON, ALCENAS or any other program, please communicate either with the ALPA Aeromedical Coordinator (Captain Ward Buckingham) or with Dr. Joseph Constantino or one of the undersigned. And should you feel an incipient problem with alcohol lies in your immediate future, don't wait for the program to be put in effect. Contact the Aeromedical Coordinator now!

We are in need of your help. It may save someone's career or, if this is no longer possible, his life.

Talk about avant-garde, in-your-face, transparent communication! And I personally knew the Chairman PAA MEC, co-author of that memorandum who himself had responded to his buddy's (my Dad!) written urging to follow Dad's example of admitting to his alcohol dependence and dealing with it like Dad had done. Recall that Dad was still flying a fulltime 747 captain's flight schedule even as he was laboring in this ALPA role, plus addressing myriad contacts from airmen all over the world, and with other airlines seeking his help with their alcohol abuse-related issues.

A directive marked "CONFIDENTIAL" and titled "ALCOHOLISM" was issued on 9/8/1976 by the Company (PAA) to flight crew for placement in their Flight Operations Administrative Manual. It reads as follows:

DEFINITION AND RELIEF

Alcoholism is a recoverable disease that can be successfully treated. The Company has a program for such treatment which is guided by the Corporate Medical Director. Any employee with a suspected drinking problem should consult with or be referred to the Corporate Medical department for examination, diagnosis and assistance in arranging for appropriate treatment as with any other illness. All medical records are treated as confidential. A word of caution: prior to committing oneself to a particular institution, it should be checked with Manager-Benefits Administration, JFK, to assure that it is on his list of accredited institutions.

EMPLOYEE BENEFITS AVAILABLE

An airman who has voluntarily consented to follow the course of treatment prescribed by the Corporate Medical Director will be eligible to avail himself of the following procedures:

1. Sick bank withdrawal to a maximum of sixty-two (62) hours per month.
2. Banked hour withdrawal to a maximum of monthly cap.
3. Liquidation of all accrued vacation time.
4. Upon liquidation of all bank and vacation credits, the individual may elect to take a Medical Leave of Absence in accordance with the then current contract provisions.
5. The group hospital benefits will be available, provided that the prescribed treatment is taken in an accredited institution.

RESTORATION TO DUTY AND FOLLOW-UP PROGRAM

An airman whose treatment requires removal from duty will be returned to duty status following satisfactory treatment as determined by the Corporate Medical Director. Restoration to flight status will be effected in the same manner as with other absences due illness. Recent findings and recommendations indicate a higher percentage of recovery is realized when a "follow-up program" is utilized after the appropriate treatment occurs. At the completion of treatment, the airman will be required to report to the Director-Flight Administration, at which time the "follow-up program" will be made known to the airman. This "follow-up program" will be presented in writing to the airman, indicating that monthly visits to the Director-Flight Administration and Medical Office and Association representative must be made. These visits will continue for a two-year period, but the period may be reduced if directed by the Medical Office. Additionally, the Medical Office may require physical examinations every six months. A note to file should be placed monthly in the airman's office jacket, confirming adherence to this program.

PENALTIES RESULTING FROM UNTREATED ALCOHOLISM

Alcoholism is a progressive disease and failure to obtain treatment invariably leads to discipline and finally to termination. A minimum penalty of six months removal from the payroll will occur whenever:

1. An airman reports for flight duty while under the influence of alcohol.

2. An airman is deemed unfit for flight duty by the Captain

or other crew members of his flight as a result of misuse of alcohol.

Termination will occur whenever:

1.An airman misuses alcohol while on flight duty.

2.An airman has twice reported for and/or been deemed unfit for flight as a result of misuse of alcohol.

An airman will, under no circumstances, be awarded medical disability coverage if his inability to perform flight duties satisfactorily is deemed by the Corporate Medical Director to have been attributable to alcoholism.

Sometimes change is resisted or muted or other-than-best, and this sterile corporate bureaucratic manifesto heightened Dad's level of frustration embodied in this October 11, 1976 mailing to the Chairman PAA MEC, quoted in part:

Since my opinions and recommendations on the proper handling of alcohol-related problems, as they may pertain to airmen, appear to be at variance with both company management and ALPA, I wish to be relieved as Chairman, MEC Prof. Stds. Comm. and Aero Medical Coordinator.

Much progress has been made in this field since 1973. However, in my opinion, the time has arrived for the next step in the proper progression of a control system. I remain ready to act in an advisory capacity to the MEC Aero Medical Coordinator to be appointed or to assist anyone individually.

Sincerely,
Ward Buckingham

PS: I enclose a copy of UAL's Assistance Program. Reference to corporate name deleted at their request lest a copy fall into the hands of sensation-seeking members of the press.

Cc: aeromedical & flight standards committees

Just one month later, November 10, 1976, the Federal Aviation Administration released an attention-getting white paper headlined ALCOHOLISM AND AIRLINE FLIGHT CREW MEMBERS. The depth of acquired insight into the disease, alcoholism, and the concern for needing a comprehensive approach to its management stands out in stark contrast to that curt bureaucratic manifesto from Company management.

Prior to this policy paper, Federal Aviation Regulations stipulated that "to be eligible for a...medical certificate, an applicant must meet the requirements" and the requirement pertaining to alcoholism read, "no established medical history or clinical diagnosis of...alcoholism." Further, an individual with such a history or diagnosis "may not act as a flight crew member, unless an exemption to the medical standards has been granted. Between 1960 and 1971, there were eight petitions from air transport pilots for exemption from the alcoholism standard. None were granted. Between 1972 and 1975, there were twenty-one such petitions of which fourteen exemptions were granted. As of September 1, there have been twenty-one exemptions for class 1 granted in 1976, with one exemption petition denied. This is a reflection of changing policy in response to adequate treatment and evaluation, appropriate selection and certain exemption limitations." This paper then devoted three paragraphs to defining alcoholism. A key segment followed, titled "INTERVENTION."

The FAA supports efforts to identify and help those flight crew members who abuse alcohol, those who might be called 'incipient' alcoholics, and those with fully developed alcoholism. These may be individuals who, on their own, become aware of their ominously increasing dependence and addiction to alcohol and wish to do something about it, or those who are identified and persuaded that they require appropriate treatment. The FAA supports the concept that alcoholism and its complications in many cases, particularly when it has not been allowed to progress to a late stage, is a disorder which can be effectively treated with a high degree of success. The recovery rate among flight crew members should be greater than that of the population in general. In those instances in which flight crew members have been granted exemption, a close and supportive monitoring system has been devised which will phase out, in most instances, at some point after a two-year period of successful rehabilitation. Alcoholism is not exclusively a chemical problem; there may be mental and emotional problems which are inextricably related to alcoholism and which must be dealt with in decisions concerning medical clearance. Prolonged alcohol abuse (and alcoholism) can also lead to temporary or chronic brain damage or other medical impairment relevant to medical qualification determinations.

The PROTOCOL FOR EXEMPTION followed:

The Federal Air Surgeon is willing to consider petitions for exemption from the medical standards received from airline flight crew members even within a month or so after they have been discharged from a qualified alcoholic rehabilitation facility or other form of appropriate intensive treatment. However, the information, in narrative summary form, obtained from an alcoholic rehabilitation facility is usually insufficient for purposes of making a determination to grant an exemption even when the information contains an examination by a psychiatrist. Experience indicated that it is prudent to obtain an independent evaluation by a qualified psychiatrist and a clinical psychologist. Only in rare cases has this proved to be unnecessary, but the unavailability of adequate consultations has frequently delayed consideration until such reports could be obtained. Therefore, in anticipation of a petition for exemption, if indicated, a flight crew member should be scheduled no sooner than 30 days after his discharge from a rehabilitation facility for psychiatric evaluation by a clinician with considerable experience in aviation psychiatry. A list of psychiatrists known to have this expertise can be provided to those involved in referrals for these consultations. It is imperative that a post-treatment psychological report (as well as any other existing reports relating to diagnosis, treatment, and rehabilitation efforts) be made available to the examining psychiatrist before he completes his evaluation. In the matter of selection of the clinical psychologist, it is perhaps simplest for the psychiatrist to assist in locating a competent, qualified clinician in his area. Psychological testing should include as a minimum some four or five tests, with the complete Wechsler Adult Intelligence Scale and Rorschach tests considered mandatory. It is suggested that the psychologist might wish to use such other tests as the Minnesota Multiphasic Personality Inventory, the 16 Personality Factor Test, the Bender-Gestalt, the Thematic Apperception Test, any form of a sentence completion test, etc. It is requested that copies of the raw test data be submitted with the psychological report.

Not much chance of 'dry-labbing' this exemption application process! I share the above detailed specifics verbatim to emphasize the magnitude of the challenge faced by the applicant flight crew member/s if they were determined to try to regain their flying privileges once grounded by the revelation of their alcoholism or alcohol abuse. And to this day airline airmen occasionally are discovered impaired on duty, having chosen to hide or deny their problem rather than capitalize on the FAA's enlightened approach to ferreting out those airmen afflicted with the disease. The Federal Air Surgeon added some concluding comments to this white paper:

It is within our capability to provide a timely decision in any fully documented case when reviewed together with the medical file from Oklahoma (the location of the Aeromedical Certification Branch of the FAA). In those certain cases which, in our opinion, do not require exemption, stipulations may nonetheless be imposed as a condition of medical qualification. In those cases which require exemption, there will be limitations which require mandatory follow-up reports from at least two sources, such as a union representative, and an air carrier representative. In addition, other qualified professionals may be requested to submit periodic reports. An individual or office not directly associated with the FAA may be designated to receive these reports, selected to fit the specific situation pertaining to the carrier and the individual. Where an air carrier medical program exists, the responsible physician (e.g. airline medical director or his designee) may be asked to perform the routine FAA medical certification examination required every six months and receive the monitoring reports. In some instances, psychiatric evaluations will be required approximately every six months. The longer there is successful remission, the less will be the need for monitoring. Accordingly, whenever possible, provisions for diminishing or even terminating the follow-up reports and psychiatric consultations will be specified in the Grant of Exemption.

While it is our function, consistent with the public safety, to render service to the individual, the Company, and various programs designed to deal with the problem of alcohol abuse and alcoholism in airmen, this is not a commitment to reach favorable determination in any case which has nominally been processed through treatment, whatever the modality. The individual case must stand on its own merit for an exemption, and be persuasive enough that the individual is committed to total abstinence and reasonably unencumbered by emotional or other health problems.

A 'slip' which occurs soon after discharge from an alcoholic rehabilitation facility is not entirely rare and would not necessarily preclude the ultimate grant of exemption, providing there followed a successful course of 'recycling' treatment. The sine qua non for continued exemption is 'total abstinence.' We do not anticipate it likely that exemption for alcoholism will be continued for an airman who is unable to maintain total abstinence. Therefore, it is important that a perceptive clinical judgment be made that the individual is firmly stabilized before his case is submitted for exemption consideration.

Meanwhile, the airline (not PAA) regional medical director shared his concerns in a white paper dated January 20, 1977 and titled "Permanent Grounding Rhetoric." It reads in part:

> The single reason why alcoholism rehabilitation programs in industry have realized some success is that of the power of the organizations to threaten an employee's economic life with the specter of separation if he refuses to cooperate and is persistently unable to perform. To eliminate this would eliminate, at the outset, the hope of influencing an individual to turn the corner in his downward course due to this affliction. Without the clout of economic threat an industrial program would be no more effective than the local minister, the family doctor, the union friend, or the helpful supervisor and so forth, working independently. We realize now, only after many years of failure, that regardless of their good intentions, single individuals or single groups of individuals have been unsuccessful. We learned the hard way that the multi-discipline approach is the optimum one. To change the grounding rhetoric would compromise that effectiveness. There is also the possibility of an individual falsely declaring to be an alcoholic in an effort to gain time or otherwise improve his economic situation. Most disturbing would be the prospect of the Company underwriting the drinking habit of an alcoholic who is able to manipulate the system. This would inevitably occur. In as much as we allude to the disease concept of alcoholism, I am convinced that this consideration has been singularly effective in changing the stigma associated with this problem.

It is apparent that Dad's letter of October 11, 1976, wherein he cited variance between himself and both company management and ALPA policy as reason for his resigning his PAA-MEC leadership positions, had major impact. I say this because on January 31, 1977, he authored the original Employee Assistance Program (EAP) formulated jointly by the Company and the union, PAA and PAA-MEC.

It had taken four years since his appointment as PAA-MEC Aeromedical Coordinator and, importantly, major change in how the FAA handled airmen afflicted with alcoholism. His 'blanket' mailing on June 25, 1976 to multiple management people for the Company and ALPA-PAA was clearly a catalyst. It read in part:

The establishment of an 'Employee Assistance Program' is imperative. I enclose information provided by the 'Milwaukee Road' tracing the development of their very effective program, which, with little modification, would fit Pan Am. I have contacted Mr. Robert Hickle, Director of Social Counseling, Milwaukee Road. He has agreed to meet with company and union representatives in New York to describe the 'nuts and bolts' for program establishment plus cost factors and investment recovery. Please arrange a conference in New York at the earliest possible time. We must insist that such a program be established. If it is not forthcoming, neither ALPA nor management has borne its responsibility to the industry, traveling public, investors or employees. Historically, the pilots have 'led the way' for the betterment of relations between management and all employees. Equipment essential to the successful accomplishment of the mission is available. Let's get on with it.

Following is that seminal EAP penned by Dad. With minor modifications, this became Pan Am's official Company program for dealing with flight crew employee alcoholism. Dad directed that the November 1976 FAA position paper titled "Alcoholism and Airline Flight Crew Members" be added to this EAP mailing:

31 Jan. 1977

The attached represents the studied opinion of the PAA MEC in the matter of the establishment of a comprehensive policy on alcoholism and an effective program for its control to be sponsored jointly by PAA and the PAA-MEC.

Ward Buckingham

MEC Aero Medical Coordinator & Professional Standards Committee Chairman

To: ALL PAN AM FLIGHT PERSONNEL

PAA (hereinafter called the Company) and the PAA employees as represented by ALPA desire to establish an Employee Assistance Program designed to assist employees with the difficulties that may ensue from alcohol dependency. Both ALPA Medical and Company Medical have been involved in the establishment of alcohol dependency programs, and it is now the desire of the Company and the ALPA to offer a program which will make the services and resources of both organizations available to employees who may have an alcohol dependency problem. The choice of facilities will be made by the employee. The Company and the ALPA recognize that alcohol dependency presents a special problem to FAA licensed airmen, and they have a mutual desire to assist in the resolution of this problem.

The Company recognizes that alcohol dependency is a disease and has made a commitment to assist employees during medical treatment and recovery. Employees suffering from alcohol dependency will receive the same medical care and sick leave benefits available for any other illness and are assured of all normal employee benefits while participating in approved medical programs under the Employee Assistance Program; furthermore they are assured of confidentiality. No employee who requests treatment for alcohol dependency will have his job security jeopardized by his request for treatment. CONFIDENTIALITY AND ASSISTANCE ARE THE ESSENTIAL INGREDIENTS IN THIS PROGRAM. Each employee must recognize the seriousness of this disease and the absolute necessity for treatment. Untreated alcohol dependency can not only cost you your job but can cost you your life. Participation in the Employee Assistance Program is the first step in controlling this dangerous disease. We earnestly solicit your 100% support.

WHAT IS THE PROGRAM?

The Employee Assistance Program is both preventive and remedial in nature. Its purpose is twofold. First, it will focus on education and early recognition and diagnosis; secondly, it will provide effective treatment to ensure rehabilitation and subsequent return to flight status. Furthermore, this Program implements authorized Company policies and procedures.

The Director Flight Operations/Chief Pilot at each pilot base will appoint one Check Airman or other qualified individual to act as Base Coordinator. The Coordinator will work in conjunction with PAA-MEC Employee Assistance Advocates (Employee Assistance Committee), pilot supervisors and Medical Departments (PAA & ALPA) to provide all possible support and assistance to airmen who may suffer from alcohol dependency. Treatment is through recognized and approved community resources. Airmen suffering from alcohol dependency will receive the same administrative and medical benefits as employees with any other illness while participating in approved medical programs under the Employee Assistance Program. The Program consists of these phases: First, it provides the means for identifying behavioral problems at an early stage. This not only makes rehabilitation easier but minimizes the damage and costs involved. The second phase of the program is to motivate the employee to accept treatment and to help him obtain the most effective treatment available. The third phase of the program consists of 'follow-up,' supervision and support to facilitate the employee's return to complete effectiveness and job efficiency. Safety and efficiency are not to be compromised by this Program. As an international air carrier, Pan Am has an obligation to operate with the highest degree of safety. It will continue to meet that standard. Supervisors are responsible for assuring that the work is properly performed. The determination as to an employee's medical capability to perform a job will be made by the PAA Medical Department in accordance with the currently effective working agreement. In addition, pilots must meet applicable federal qualifications for the job.

This is a 'people program.' Mutual trust, faith and sincerity are required for its success.

EMPLOYEE ALCOHOL DEPENDENCY POLICY

1. The company recognizes alcoholism as an illness which can be successfully treated by means of existing therapeutic methods. Experience in many large companies has shown that a large percentage of employees suffering from alcohol dependence can achieve successful recovery with proper help and treatment.

2. The Company's concern with alcoholism is strictly limited to its effects on the employee's relationship with the Company. It is not concerned with social drinking. Whether an employee without alcoholism chooses to drink or not to drink socially is of concern only to the individual. Flight personnel are reminded of their responsibility to observe Company and FAA regulations. The Employee Assistance Program for flight personnel has two purposes: first, it will focus on education in order to promote early diagnosis, and second, it will be geared to providing effective treatment to ensure rehabilitation and subsequent return to flight status. Employees suffering from alcohol dependency will receive the same medical care and sick leave benefits available for any other illness and are assured of all normal employee benefits while

participating in approved medical programs under the Employee Assistance Program. The disability income replacement benefits will not be paid in the case of permanent grounding of an airman due to alcoholism. No airman may be returned to active status until he has undergone appropriate treatment and received medical clearance.

3. For the purpose of this policy, alcohol dependency is defined as an illness in which an employee's consumption of any alcoholic beverage <u>might now or in the future</u> interfere with his job performance and/or his health. The Company intends that the same careful consideration now given to all of our employees having other illnesses will be extended to employees having alcohol dependency. The social stigma often associated with this illness has no basis in fact, and it is expected that this enlightened attitude and realistic acceptance of alcohol dependency as an illness will encourage employees to take advantage of the available treatment whenever needed. The Company recognizes that by the nature and description of the disease, the employee will seldom seek diagnosis or treatment of his own volition, and that assistance from his peer group and/or his supervisor will be necessary and desirable.

4. It is expected that through this policy, employees who suspect they may have an alcohol associated problem, even in its early stages, will be encouraged to seek diagnosis and, when indicated, follow through with the prescribed treatment.

5. After a diagnosis of alcohol dependency has been made, during inpatient treatment or under a medical regimen requiring drugs, flight crew members will not continue to work due to job and medical certification requirements. Such employees will receive applicable sick leave and medical benefits while off the job undergoing prescribed treatments. Flight crew members will be returned to work to the extent they are medically and legally qualified to do so.

6. It is recognized that supervisors do not have the professional qualifications to permit judgment as to whether or not an employee suffers from alcohol dependency. Supervisor referrals for diagnosis and treatment may be based on an unsatisfactory dependability record or other information which might indicate an underlying problem.

7. ALPA has an operating program on alcohol dependency and has established an Employee Assistance Committee (comprised of employee assistance advocates) as a PAA-MEC function. This organization will act in concert with the PAA Alcohol Assistance Program to insure that the full resources of both organizations are used to achieve the highest possible recovery rate. Referral to either Company or ALPA treatment resources will be the airman's decision. It will be the responsibility of the employee to comply with referrals for diagnosis and to cooperate fully with the prescribed therapy. An employee's refusal to accept diagnosis, treatment, reassessments, or failure to respond to treatment or reassessment will be handled in exactly the same way similar refusals or treatment failures are handled for other illnesses. Responsibility for final evaluation will lie with the PAA Medical Department, in accordance with the current effective working agreement (labor contract).

8. The confidential nature of the medical records of airmen employees with alcohol dependency will be assured in the same manner as medical records pertaining to other diseases. However, it is recognized that there may be an exchange of necessary information between the ALPA Medical Department and the PAA Medical Department in order to expedite the return of the recovering airman to flight status.

9. This policy should not be construed as condoning any lowering of standards applicable to proper job performance. Supervisors are responsible for monitoring job performance in the customary manner to assure that applicable standards are met. No special privileges or exemptions from normal counseling or disciplinary procedures are to be accorded employees who fail to meet work standards or who violate Company regulations.

10. The Company recognizes the unique problems of the FAA licensed employee created by federal medical certification requirements. The Company pledges to assist in securing medical recertification following successful treatment. To that end the publication of November 10, 1976 by the FAA titled 'ALCOHOLISM AND AIRLINE FLIGHT CREW MEMBERS' as it may be revised is made part of this policy.

11. The program will be reviewed at least annually in order to incorporate necessary changes as they may become evident.

THE SUPERVISOR

In dealing with behavioral problems, the Supervisor must restrict any criticism to job performance itself. These are the responsibilities the Supervisor must keep in mind.

1. The Supervisor should be alert for any evidence of changing attendance patterns or other information which might indicate an underlying problem, even if there is no indication of deterioration of health or job performance.

2. The Supervisor should not attempt to distinguish or diagnose the cause of problems brought to his attention. However, he should know the facts: (a) alcoholism is an illness, (b) it is progressive, (c) delayed action can result in the loss of the employee, in severe physical deterioration, and early death.

3. The Supervisor should be aware that assistance is available if he suspects a problem of alcohol dependence. He should consult the Base Coordinator, who in turn will request assistance from the Employee Assistance Advocate. These men should seek the assistance of the PAA Medical Department in planning the best approach to the employee.

4. The Supervisor, or if he chooses to delegate the responsibility, the Base Coordinator and the appropriate Employee Assistance Advocate will have the initial face-to-face talk with the employee. The management representative will review the problem and counsel the employee that if remedial action is not taken, discipline may result. The suggestion should be made that the employee visit the Medical Department.

5. After an employee has received the prescribed treatment and has been returned to duty, the Supervisor should participate with the Base Coordinator, MEC Employee Assistance Advocate, and PAA Medical in a follow-up program to provide support and assistance for the rehabilitated employee. Involvement in A.A. appears to provide the most effective means of maintaining abstinence. The follow-up program may be instrumental in preventing a relapse.

The Supervisor will continue his normal supervisory relationship and continue to monitor the employee's job performance, taking action consistent with standard disciplinary procedures when job performance is affected. In case of incidents involving rules violations, appropriate discipline should be applied in the normal manner.

THE BASE COORDINATOR

The duties and responsibilities of the coordinator shall include:

1. To work closely and confidentially with the MEC Employee Assistance Advocates, the pilot's supervisor and Medical Departments (Company and ALPA) whenever a suspected alcohol dependency problem exists, at all times keeping in mind the best interests of the pilot involved.

2. To become educated regarding alcohol and alcoholism (Johnson Institute or other NCA recommended facility)

3. To provide counseling to supervisors in order to assist them in dealing with individual employees who may be afflicted with a medical or behavioral problem

4. Make recommendations to the supervisor involved regarding strategy of motivational action in specific cases.

5. To refrain from diagnosing alcoholism, and to remember at all times that he is neither an alcohol counselor nor a medical doctor, but to refer employees to the Medical Department when appropriate.

6. Help employees receive all assistance provided by the joint PAA-ALPA program.

7. Maintain continuing follow-up and status of individual cases.

8. To keep any information regarding any particular case in STRICTEST CONFIDENCE sharing on a 'need-to-know' basis only when necessary.

9. To handle each referral as necessary and as indicated under the PAA-ALPA Employee Assistance Program.

EMPLOYEE ASSISTANCE ADVOCATE

1. At least one designated for each base by the PAA-MEC through the MEC Aero Medical Coordinator and Professional Standards Chairman.

2. May or may not serve as local Aero Medical Coordinator and Professional Standards Chairman.

3. Must be qualified through attendance at HIMS Seminars, ALPA Denver, conducted for that purpose, or at other appropriate facilities such as the Johnson Institute etc.

4. Where possible he/she should be a recovering alcoholic with adequate longevity in sobriety.

5. At the outset, education of all airmen is essential. Maintaining a highly visible position as the Employee Assistance Advocate is imperative.

6. Will participate with Supervisor and/or Base Coordinator in intervention procedure.

7. Consult with HIMS Director, Denver, when warranted.

8. Offer full support and counsel to the affected employee in order to assure his return to flying status in an appropriately expeditious manner.

9. Monitor follow-up as necessary.

10. Will keep information regarding all cases in strictest confidence sharing on a "need to know" basis only when necessary

MEDICAL DEPARTMENT RESPONSIBILITIES

The Company Medical Department will:

1. Define a program for medical diagnosis and recovery.

2. Develop medical guidelines for the referral of employee problems to the appropriate agency.

3. Develop a list of approved facilities whose rehabilitation programs have been determined to be the best available.

4. Using the recommendation of NCA, arrange for the showing of pertinent educational films during airmen's semi-annual training periods.

All of this information will be shared with the ALPA Medical Department and the PAA-MEC Employee Assistance Advocates to enable the two groups to work in close cooperation to solve any alcohol associated problems among PAA airmen which might be brought to the attention of ALPA or PAA. In addition, the PAA Medical Department will cooperate with the ALPA Medical Department to establish protocol which will facilitate medical recertification.

Since the aims of ALPA Medical are the same as PAA Medical, there may be a full exchange of medical information pertaining to the Employee Assistance Program.

EMPLOYEE ASSISTANCE PROGRAM ADMINISTRATOR
Qualifications:

1. Experience in organization and administration of successful alcoholism recovery programs.

2. Education and experience in alcoholism counseling.

3. Background in aviation and familiarity with idiosyncrasies of the federal bureaucracy.

4. Preferably a recovering alcoholic. If not, have a proven feel for the disease.

Duties:

1. Provide overall administration of the Employee Assistance Program

2. Maintain records showing program cost recovery and overall efficacy of program.

3. Visit each base bimonthly to educate involved personnel.

4. Maintain liaison between PAA, the unions and treatment centers utilized.

5. Be prepared to expand the program for flight personnel to include all PAA employees.

6. Responsible directly to the Corporate President and Chief operating Officer.

ATTACHMENT

From: Federal Aviation Administration, Washington D.C. Nov.10, 1976

ALCOHOLISM AND AIRLINE FLIGHT CREW MEMBERS

Part 67 of the Federal Aviation Regulations pertaining to Medical Standards and Certification states: 'To be eligible for a medical certificate, an applicant must meet the requirements...' The requirement pertaining to alcoholism is: 'No established medical history or clinical diagnosis of alcoholism.'

An individual who has a medical history or clinical diagnosis of alcoholism does not meet the medical standards and may not act as a flight crew member, unless an exemption to the medical standards has been granted.

Between 1960 and 1971, there were eight petitions from air transport pilots for exemption from the alcoholism standard. None were granted. Between 1972 and 1975, there were twenty-one such petitions of which fourteen exemptions were granted. As of September 1, there have been twenty-one exemptions for class I granted in 1976, with one exemption petition denied. This is a reflection of changing policy in response to adequate treatment and evaluation, appropriate selection and certain exemption limitations.

61

DIAGNOSIS

Alcoholism, as currently defined, is a diagnosable disease in those whose intake is great enough to damage physical health or personal or social functioning (which includes occupational functioning) or when it has become a prerequisite to normal functioning (Diagnostic and Statistical Manual of Mental Disorders, 2nd Edition (DSM-12), 1968; Federal Aviation Regulations, Part 67).

Since alcoholism is usually characterized by an evolutionary development preceded by a long period of increasing abuse, there may not be a precisely identifiable point in time beyond which an individual is clearly an 'alcoholic.' As a consequence, there is often some justifiable confusion in differentiating between alcohol abuse and alcoholism. At the very least, serious concern is warranted if one is at the point of attempting to make this distinction.

While there may be an overlapping range between incipient alcoholism and alcoholism, which often presents a differential diagnostic challenge in which there is room for differing clinical opinions, there are certain objective criteria which are either so strongly suggestive or pathognomonic of alcoholism that they cannot be ignored. Some of these criteria would be: (1) a history of more than one arrest for driving while intoxicated; (2) the need for medical detoxification; (3) the development of neuropathy; (4) alcoholic psychoses, including delirium tremens; or (5) seizures on withdrawal.

INTERVENTION

The FAA supports efforts to identify and help those flight crew members who abuse alcohol, those who might be called 'incipient alcoholics,' and those with fully developed alcoholism. These may be individuals who, on their own, become aware of their ominously increasing dependence and addiction to alcohol and wish to do something about it, or those who are identified and persuaded that they require appropriate treatment.

The FAA supports the concept that alcoholism and its complications in many cases, particularly when it has not been allowed to progress to a late stage, is a disorder which can be effectively treated with a high degree of success. The recovery rate among flight crew members should be greater than that of the population in general. In those instances in which flight crew members have been granted exemption, a close and supportive monitoring system has been devised which will phase out, in most instances, at some point after a two-year period of successful rehabilitation. Alcoholism is not exclusively a chemical problem; there may be mental and emotional problems which are inextricably related to alcoholism and which must be dealt with in decisions concerning medical clearance. Prolonged alcohol abuse (and alcoholism) can also lead to temporary or chronic brain damage or other medical impairment relevant to medical qualification determinations.

PROTOCOL FOR EXEMPTION

The Federal Air Surgeon is willing to consider petitions for exemption from the medical standards received from airline flight crew members even within a month or so after they have been discharged from a qualified alcoholic rehabilitation facility or other form of appropriate intensive treatment. However, the information, in narrative summary form, obtained from an alcoholic rehabilitation facility is usually insufficient for purposes of making a determination to grant an exemption even when the information contains an examination by a psychiatrist. Experience indicates that it is prudent to obtain an independent evaluation by a qualified psychiatrist and a clinical psychologist. Only in rare cases has this proved to be unnecessary, but the unavailability of adequate consultations has frequently delayed consideration until such reports could be obtained. Therefore, in anticipation of a petition for exemption, if indicated, a flight crew member should be scheduled no sooner than 30 days after his discharge from a rehabilitation facility for psychiatric evaluation by a clinician with considerable experience in aviation psychiatry. A list of psychiatrists known to have this expertise can be provided to those involved in referrals for these consultations.

It is imperative that a post-treatment psychological report (as well as any other existing reports relating to diagnosis, treatment, and rehabilitation efforts) be made available to the examining psychiatrist before he completes his evaluation. In the matter of selection of the clinical psychologist, it is perhaps simplest for the psychiatrist to assist in locating a competent, qualified clinician in his area. Psychological testing should include as a minimum some four or five tests, with the complete Wechsler Adult Intelligence Scale and Rorschach tests considered mandatory. It is suggested that the psychologist might wish to use such other tests as the

Minnesota Multiphasic Personality Inventory, the 16 Personality Factor Test, the Bender-Gestalt, the Thematic Apperception Test, any form of a sentence completion test, etc. It is requested that copies of the raw test data be submitted with the psychological report.

With the above protocol in mind, a completed case should be forwarded directly to Jon L. Jordan, M.D., Chief, AeroMedical Standards Division, AAM-200, Office of Aviation Medicine, Federal Aviation Administration, Washington D.C. 20591, along with a current application/report of medical examination (FAA Form 8500-8). An information copy of any covering letter to Dr. Jordan should be sent to Audie W. Davis, M.D., Chief, AeroMedical Certification Branch, AAC-130, FAA Aeronautical Center, P.O.Box 25082, Oklahoma City, Oklahoma 73125, so that Dr. Davis can expedite the transmission of the airman's FAA medical file to Washington. In addition, the package should include a written request by the airman, or his designated representative, for exemption consideration.

FEDERAL AIR SURGEON ACTION

It is within our capability to provide a timely decision in any fully documented case when reviewed together with the medical file from Oklahoma. In those certain cases which, in our opinion, do not require exemption, stipulations may nonetheless be imposed as a condition of medical qualification. In those cases which require exemption, there will be limitations which require mandatory follow-up reports from at least two sources, such as a union representative, and an air carrier representative. In addition, other qualified professionals may be requested to submit periodic reports. An individual or office not directly associated with the FAA may be designated to receive these reports, selected to fit the specific situation pertaining to the carrier and the individual. Where an air carrier medical program exists, the responsible physician (e.g. airline medical director or his designee) may be asked to perform the routine FAA medical certification examination required every six months and receive the monitoring reports. In some instances, psychiatric evaluations will be required approximately every six months. The longer there is successful remission, the less will be the need for monitoring. Accordingly, whenever possible, provisions for diminishing or even terminating the follow-up reports and psychiatric consultations will be specified in the Grant of Exemption.

While it is our function, consistent with the public safety, to render service to the individual, the company, and various programs designed to deal with the problem of alcohol abuse and alcoholism in airmen, this is not a commitment to reach favorable determinations in any case which has nominally been processed through treatment, whatever the modality. The individual case must stand on its own merit for an exemption and be persuasive enough that the individual is committed to total abstinence and reasonably unencumbered by emotional or other health problems.

A 'slip' which occurs soon after discharge from an alcoholic rehabilitation facility is not entirely rare and would not necessarily preclude the ultimate grant of exemption, providing there followed a successful course of 'recycling' treatment. The sine qua non for continued exemption is 'total abstinence.' We do not anticipate it likely that exemption for alcoholism will be continued for an airman who is unable to maintain total abstinence. Therefore, it is important that a perceptive clinical judgment be made that the individual is firmly stabilized before his case is submitted for exemption consideration.

CHAPTER FIVE
EXEMPTION FOR ALCOHOLISM & ALCOHOL EFFECTS ON FLYING SKILL

The phrase "timing is everything" may seem trite but it certainly fits here. Reflect on the sequence of events from September's Company 'manifesto' to Dad's October resignation letter to FAA's November paper (Alcoholism and Airline Flight Crew Members) to Dad's seminal Employee Assistance Program paper adopted (with minor changes) by the Company in February.

Dad's friend with United Airlines had just been successful in obtaining an FAA exemption after 13 years of sobriety, leading Dad to believe his 11 years of sobriety plus the newly spelled out FAA policy created a favorable atmosphere for 'coming out' to acquire exemption status. As if the powers that be were ignorant of his past history of alcoholism? Apparently, it had been carefully omitted from any part of his written health record with the FAA. Dr. Francis Schwartz, UAL's regional medical director, was one of those contacted by Dad to assist in the exemption application process. Following is the letter Dr. Schwartz sent to the PAA medical director on Dad's behalf dated March 14, 1977:

> Captain Buckingham stopped by the office Friday afternoon indicating that he was interested in requesting an exemption for alcoholism from the Federal Air Surgeon. Knowing that we supported one of our own retired alcoholic captains in a petition for exemption, he requested that I forward a copy of my letter to the Air Surgeon to you. The pilot in question, Capt. _____
>
> _____, has given me permission to forward this to you. I have the AA underground to thank for my introduction to Ward Buckingham, which came better than three years ago. At the time we were involved in what seemed like perpetual talks preliminary to beginning an active program for rehabilitation. Buck was good enough to sit in with us and his effort turned the trick in getting us into action. For that he must be considered a serious contributor to what we are doing. He was a founder of the original "Birds of a Feather" AA group in Seattle. As you know, this movement is catching on internationally as a singularly effective instrument in the recovery of aviators. In addition, he assisted the local Bay Area group to begin a chapter a year ago. The help this chapter has given our pilots is not difficult to measure. It has been stupendous and we would be truly lost without it. It would be foolhardy to attempt to identify single individuals responsible for a movement as complex as rehabilitation of alcoholics. In my estimation, on a national and even international basis, Ward Buckingham was in

the middle of it. We are deeply indebted to this man for his assistance and I am elated to have the opportunity to thank him formally even though the route is somewhat obtuse. His recovery is as firm as any of the remarkable people I have had the privilege of knowing.

(Note: blank line represents name omitted by me consistent with AA practice)

Dad himself wrote the following on March 21, 1977, to Dr. Frederick Leeds, PAA Medical Director:

Regarding our conversation on March 15 concerning disclosure to the Federal Air Surgeon of my 'Problem Drinking' history, I present the following in more or less narrative form. It became apparent to me in 1965 that drinking was interfering with the orderly progression of my life. During my recovery from surgery performed the latter part of 1965 I joined Alcoholics Anonymous and have been continuously abstinent since January 12, 1966. I did not at that time disclose my 'Problem Drinking' to the FAA since I knew disqualification would result for at least 2 years (more probably permanent disqualification would result), to the good of no one. I was determined to remain abstinent through association with A.A. and remain 'in the woodwork' until a more healthy climate for disclosure became extant. At no time during my 'drinking career' did I become involved with the 'law.' At no time did I fail to accomplish proficiency checks or training for upgrade. I was, on occasion, admonished by my supervisor to 'watch my drinking.' Dissatisfaction with the direction in which my life was proceeding was the motivating force for me to secure a more satisfactory existence. You are aware of my involvement in the alcohol recovery programs in the field of aviation, both the union and management positions. I request that you make representations in my behalf before the Federal Air Surgeon.

Dr. Leeds composition on Dad's behalf is dated April 28, 1977, and was directed to Dr. Jon Jordan, Chairman, Aeromedical Standards Division of the FAA. His writing reads in part as follows:

Captain Buckingham's history of having had a problem with alcohol prior to 1966 did not come to my attention until the last four or five years. It came to my attention via Captain Buckingham himself and his close association with me over the past approximately four years relative to his acting as an advisor to me in our formulation of an alcoholism prevention program. In the latter capacity, I have had numerous and frequent contacts with

67

Captain Buckingham which have been extremely valuable to me relative to our overall program, and through these contacts it has been more than obvious to me that Captain Buckingham has maintained total abstinence since his last drink on January 12, 1966. He has, in my opinion, proven beyond a doubt that he has long since recovered from any drinking problem he may have had in the past. I consider him an authority in the field, particularly as it relates to airline pilots. As you may know, he was a founder of the original 'Birds of a Feather' AA group in Seattle and has been a leader in this movement, as well as extensive involvement in other efforts to aid in the rehabilitation of alcoholics. Prior to, and of course since 1966, Captain Buckingham has at no time been involved in any incidents relative to drinking. He has had no problems with his work as an airline pilot or with his proficiency checks or training for upgrading. He originally became involved with AA on a voluntary basis because he realized, much to his credit, that the direction of his life would be much more constructive without alcohol. In summary, his record of sobriety speaks for itself, and I would recommend him for exemption without reservation.

Copies of the above were also directed by Dr. Leeds to both Dr. Audie Davis, Chief, Aeromedical Certification Branch-FAA, and Dr. Reighard, Federal Air Surgeon-FAA. The third reference on his behalf was provided by Dr. Richard Masters, principal investigator of the ALPA's Human Intervention and Motivation Study (HIMS) and its medical advisor:

Dear Dr. Reighard:

As you know, Captain Ward Buckingham, Pan American Airways (PAA), has elected to declare his belief that he is an alcoholic person at the National Council on Alcoholism meeting at San Diego on April 30, 1977. By your previous telephone conversations, you know that he has asked that I relate to you my feelings regarding his sobriety and actions. While I have no detailed medical history pertaining to his case, I have known Ward since 1972 and have worked closely with him many times in conjunction with his duties as Aeromedical Coordinating Committee Chairman, PAA. Additionally, I have had opportunities to work with him on a personal basis when he has participated in training seminars for ALPA aeromedical coordinators and, later, in the formative work leading to the development of the ALPA HIMS program. Ward has been an invaluable advisor to me and the HIMS staff and I consider him to be most knowledgeable in the area of alcoholism. Virtually single-handedly, Ward has spear-headed the formalization and maturation of a working alcohol rehabilitation program on his own airline, and his leadership has gained the respect of all concerned. Perhaps an even more important activity has been his work in developing 'Birds of a Feather' Alcoholics Anonymous programs in several metropolitan areas of the country. The 'Birds' groups are well known to provide superlative recovery-strengthening programs, allowing pilots to relate to peers in working through their specialized problems. Hence, Ward has been a tireless worker for PAA pilots as well as brother airline pilots. I am completely comfortable with the sobriety and serenity of Captain Buckingham and firmly believe he is fully qualified for uninterrupted unrestricted medical certification. If I can be of further assistance, please call on me.

On June 17, 1977, which was 11 years after achieving permanent sobriety and nine months before mandatory flight retirement at age 60, formal exemption for his history of alcoholism was granted by the FAA (see following two-page document copy). Dad was personally gratified to be on the receiving end of fundamental change in the FAA's flight certification for airmen like him with alcoholism histories. As founder of Birds of a Feather, he extended an invite personally to Federal Air Surgeon Reighard to attend and speak at Seattle BOAF second anniversary meeting December 1977. Los Angeles and San Francisco 'Birds' attended as well, and all assembled demonstrated their appreciation to this FAA leader with a standing ovation for Dr. Reighard and his presentation to them. I can't resist adding a kudo to Dad provided in 1978 by the same Dr. Francis Schwartz whose earlier letter I quoted above. He authored a paper titled "Method for Rehabilitation of the Alcohol-Addicted Pilot in a Commercial Airline" published in the May 1978 issue of "Aviation, Space and Environmental Medicine." On the front page of that article reprint sent by Dr. Schwartz to Dad is the handwritten note: "To Captain Buck---without whose benefaction this Phoenix would never have left the drawing board. With my greatest admiration. Frank." Dad's input on the final United Airlines Employee Assistance Program for alcoholic pilots was recognized as key during those transformative years. But also notable is the fact that a United Airlines memorandum to "ALL UNITED PILOTS" dated September 1, 1976, has Dad's penciled modifications for what Pan Am would shortly thereafter circulate to their pilots. It dealt with the newly open topic of alcohol dependency among pilots (although UAL had fledgling efforts in this arena going back to 1968).

UNITED STATES OF AMERICA
DEPARTMENT OF TRANSPORTATION
FEDERAL AVIATION ADMINISTRATION
WASHINGTON, D.C. 20591

```
* * * * * * * * * * * * * * * * *
                                 *
In the matter of the petition of *
                                 *
WARD BUCKINGHAM                  *
                                 *         Regulatory Docket No. 16949
for an exemption from certain    *
provisions of Part 67 of the     *
Federal Aviation Regulations     *
                                 *
* * * * * * * * * * * * * * * * *
```

GRANT OF EXEMPTION

By petition dated April 29, 1977, Ward Buckingham, 2600 SW. 167th Place,
Seattle, Washington 98166, requested an exemption from section
67.13(d)(1)(i)(c) of Federal Aviation Regulations Part 67 (disqualifying
an applicant with an established medical history or clinical diagnosis
of alcoholism), for the issuance of a first-class airman medical certificate. The request for exemption is based on the grounds that petitioner
believes that his medical condition would not interfere with his safe
performance of the airman duties to which his petition refers.

The medical evidence submitted shows that petitioner's health would
permit the safe performance of pertinent airman duties under the conditions stated herein. In light of the specific situation involved, I
therefore find that the grant of the requested exemption would be in the
public interest. Therefore, pursuant to the authority contained in
sections 313(a) and 601(c) of the Federal Aviation Act of 1958 delegated
to me by the Administrator (14CFR 11.53), Ward Buckingham is granted an
exemption from section 67.13(d)(1)(i)(c) of Federal Aviation Regulations
Part 67, and a first-class airman medical certificate shall be issued to
him if he qualifies medically in all other respects, subject to the
following conditions:

  1. This exemption is limited to the specific disqualifying medical
condition noted above.

  2. Petitioner shall promptly report any adverse change in his
medical condition to: FAA Aeronautical Center, Aeromedical Certification Branch (AAC-130), P.O. Box 25082, Oklahoma City, Oklahoma 73125.

3. Medical certificates issued pursuant to this exemption shall be endorsed as follows:

>Limited by conditions in exemption from FAR's
>section 67.13(d)(1)(i)(c). Exemption No. M-10590
>dated   JUN 1 7 1977

4. Upon notice thereof to the petitioner, this exemption and any medical certificate issued pursuant thereto shall terminate if the Federal Air Surgeon finds that there has been a substantial adverse change in any aspect of petitioner's medical condition. Such action shall not preclude petitioner from requesting exemption in the future, on the basis of a new petition.

5. Under the terms of this exemption, future medical certificates may be issued by an FAA-designated Aviation Medical Examiner on the basis of appropriate physical examinations. Such medical certificates shall bear the legend specified in Condition 3 of this Grant of Exemption, in addition to an appropriate lens requirement.

Petitioner's first-class medical certificate is enclosed. This supersedes and replaces the medical certificate issued by Dr. Fred A. Ellis on March 15, 1977.

H. L. Reighard, M.D.

Federal Air Surgeon, AAM-1

Issued in Washington, D.C. on JUN 1 7 1977

Enclosure

As if he wasn't busy enough with full flight schedule and ALPA leadership roles and this application for FAA exemption process, Dad delivered the following prepared remarks before the National Council on Alcoholism annual meeting in San Diego on April 30, 1977, his first prominent public declaration of being an alcoholic:

> The presence of two airline pilots at this momentous gathering should not be construed to indicate that alcoholism is endemic to or of epidemic proportions in the ranks of the nation's airline crews. Our presence serves to prove that although finely screened, highly trained, scrutinized and controlled, we are still human.

> Until the very recent past an airman who fell victim to the disease was terminated and wound down to an unpleasant and untimely death. In my opinion alcohol and the pathologies associated with its abuse constitute the largest cause for early termination of airmen careers. Those of us who were fortunate enough to secure help in arresting the progression of the disease remained 'in the woodwork' lest the word get out and identify us as 'one of those.' This was mandatory if we wished to continue in the profession we revere. Alcoholism is disqualifying under part 67 of the Federal Aviation Regulations, thus requiring an exemption to those regulations for medical certification. Until the latter part of 1972, no exemptions were granted. This underlined the necessity for our remaining 'in the woodwork' and maintaining a low profile, awaiting a more favorable climate.

> That climate has arrived in the person of the Federal Air Surgeon, H. L. Reighard and his staff. Exemptions are now being granted subject to the satisfaction of certain stringent conditions. Their enlightened approach to the solution of this difficult problem is to be highly commended.

> All of the foregoing brings us to the question: why am I present at this gathering? As has been said, 'eternal vigilance is the price of freedom.' For me, continued association with the winners is the price I must pay for my continuous happy sobriety. I enjoy paying the price.

Stop to consider for a moment. Dad had been permanently sober for 11 years, been making himself available to others far and wide in need of help with alcoholism, been an activist leader regarding alcohol and airmen through the ALPA and airline industry for five years, but only now felt his flying job secure enough (with respect to FAA certification policy) to publicly declare his alcoholism past in a national forum.

The National Institute of Alcohol Abuse and Alcoholism (NIAAA), an arm of U. S. Department of Health Education and Welfare, published a relevant white paper March 3, 1978 titled "Program Fosters Recovery of Alcoholic Pilots." This pointed out that ALPA served as both professional association and collective bargaining agent for some 30,000 pilot-members employed by 35 airlines at that time. As of this paper's publication, approximately 23 airlines were in the process of developing formal programs for dealing with alcoholic airmen. In the first 30 months of ALPA's tie with alcoholism assistance programs, approximately 250 pilots received advice or assistance. Fourteen percent of those were self-referrals while 72 % were peer-referrals. During that same period, 74 pilots like Dad applied for recertification through this NIAAA-sponsored program. Fifty-nine of the 74 received the medical endorsement of the ALPA program office, and all but one were recertified by the FAA. Although the follow-up duration to the time of this paper had been relatively short, it is interesting to note that 52 of those recertified maintained sobriety while the seven who returned to drinking were "off-flight" status and in some further stage of rehabilitation. One indication of the ALPA program's impact throughout the airline industry was the growing number of pilots seeking help via channels other than the ALPA project, mainly through individual airline programs.

A very concise well-written paper by Dr. Barton Pakull, Office of Aviation Medicine-Behavioral Sciences Division, FAA, appeared in the January 1978 issue of the journal, Alcoholism: Clinical and Experimental Research. Under the title, "Alcoholism and Aviation Medical Certification," Pakull stated there were 98 petitions in 1976 with a history of alcoholism, and 77 exemptions were granted. The crucial question for a prospective applicant with a history of alcoholism, or to professionals in the field of alcohol rehabilitation is: "On what basis does the Federal Air Surgeon grant or deny an exemption to the petitioner with a history of alcoholism?" He went on to emphasize "years of abstinence" as key in the consultants' deliberations. "Other factors that are also considered are the severity of the problem and how long it existed; the age of onset and evidence of stability and adjustment before the onset of alcoholism; the number of times that treatment was sought and relapse occurred; the quality of the final treatment effort; the presence of residual medical complications, especially neurologic manifestations; and evidence of progress in marital, social, vocational and educational areas (as appropriate) since rehabilitation has begun." In other words, they look at the *whole person.*

When appropriate they also look at demonstrated commitment to rehabilitation, and they look for underlying personality difficulties that may be disqualifying or may impair sustained abstinence. In general, the longer the period of abstinence from alcohol use, the better the chances for a grant of exemption. He stated it is unusual to be granted an exemption with less than two years of abstinence, but "few petitioners fail to receive an exemption with a history of over five years of abstinence." For those applicants whose petition for exemption is denied, appeal to the National Transportation Safety Board and beyond to Federal Court remain as options. Pakull cited two commonly voiced criticisms of this process:

> 1) it unfairly penalizes an individual who has admitted to having a problem with alcohol and has sought rehabilitation, and 2) it rewards current alcoholics or those with severe alcohol problems by allowing these individuals to fly (maintain their medical certificate). In answer to the latter, we must emphasize that denials for a history of alcoholism are by no means limited to people with an 'old history.' Whenever and by whatever means it comes to the attention of the FAA that a person may have a problem with alcohol, the FAA will take steps to document the evidence and request that the individual supply copies of hospitalizations that have previously not been submitted, or the FAA may ask for a current medical evaluation. Often, the initial information comes from anonymous sources close to the airman who are concerned for the airman's personal safety, as well as aviation safety. The FAA will not act on such information unless it is confirmed. Arrests for alcohol-related offenses and unrevealed medical treatments are the most common causes for FAA action in this area. The answer to the first criticism is inherent in the difficulties of defining rehabilitation. A 'history of alcoholism' may be 2 months old or 20 years ago. No two individuals are completely alike, and it would be nearly impossible to write a satisfactory regulation that could define when an individual is medically safe to return to flying. Individual consideration would seem to be the fairest way to deal with this issue.

There is good reason to study alcohol's effect on airplane operation. Like automobile fatality crash statistics showing a substantial portion involve alcohol-impaired drivers, general aviation fatality crashes involve pilots with measurable blood alcohol levels 35% of the time (ref: Harper CR. Alcohol and general aviation accidents. Aerosp Med 1964; 35: 462-464). That figure may give a somewhat falsely high percentage because cases where alcohol is produced after death by tissue decomposition were not considered. More recent FAA data suggest about 13 % of general aviation fatalities involve pilots with BAC of 0.02 % or more. A disproportionate number of these alcohol-related aviation crashes occur at night.

Alcohol is a primary and continuous depressant of the central nervous system. Flying an aircraft in the rapidly changing three-dimensional environment of the cockpit requires high level orientation, vigilance and psychomotor coordination. Variables including navigational and engine performance instruments, radio communications, other air traffic, and aircraft attitudinal and directional control all demand nearly simultaneous monitoring to maintain safe flight. Impairment of a person's visual control of nystagmic eye movements (oculovestibular function) after vestibular stimulation similar to that encountered during normal flight (i.e. simulated pitch, yaw, roll and accelerative forces) shows up at blood alcohol concentrations (BAC) of 0.03-0.05%. These low BAC levels have little or no noticeable effect on tasks performed preparing for flight. Disruption of oculovestibular function during flight predictably decreases perception of aircraft's attitude, visual fixation and tracking ability---thus impairing the affected pilot's ability to control the aircraft, read aircraft instruments and navigational charts, and see and avoid other aircraft. Progressively higher BAC levels, not surprisingly, produce larger and more consistent reductions in all these flight control measures (ref. Modell JG,MountzJM. Drinking and Flying: the problem of alcohol use by pilots. New Engl J Med 1990; 323:455-461). These adverse effects are more pronounced at low ambient light levels such as occur during night flying. BAC levels as low as 0.015% may reduce ability to perform complex psychomotor tasks during the rapid absorption phase after ingesting alcohol (ref: Klein et al. Int Z Angew Physiol 1967; 24: 254-267). Perhaps surprising is the fact that pilots who consume large alcohol quantities many hours before flying, and whose BAC may have fallen to near zero, still show decreases in precision and accuracy in all variables tested.

The FAA published a white paper in 1994 titled "Alcohol and Flying." The expressed reason for this paper given in its introduction: "There is a tendency to forget that flying an aircraft is a highly demanding cognitive and psychomotor task that takes place in an inhospitable environment where pilots are exposed to various sources of stress." Basic facts regarding alcohol and the human body followed: 1) alcohol is rapidly absorbed and its toxic effects vary---influenced by gender, body weight, rate of consumption and total amount consumed, 2) the average healthy person eliminates alcohol at a fairly constant rate of one drink per hour (i.e. 4 oz. wine or 12 oz. light beer or 1 oz. vodka or 1.25 oz. whiskey)---thus the more alcohol consumed the longer it takes the body to eliminate it (standard alcohol-containing drink in US has 15 gm alcohol and alcohol is normally metabolized at the rate of 8 gm per hour; hence more accurate to state that *the average healthy person eliminates alcohol at a fairly constant rate of one drink every two hours*---personal communication J G Modell) , 3) undesirable effects labeled "hangover" can last 48 to 72 hours after the last drink ingested, 4) most adverse effects produced by alcohol relate to the brain, the eyes, and the inner ear---three crucial organs to the pilot, 5) brain effects include impaired reaction time, reasoning, judgment, and memory which can be magnified by exposure to altitude and a decreased partial pressure of oxygen, 6) visual symptoms include eye muscle imbalance with resulting double vision and difficulty focusing, 7) inner ear effects include dizziness and decreased hearing perception, 8) other variables like sleep deprivation , fatigue, medication use, altitude hypoxia, and flying at night or in bad weather all can magnify the negative effects listed above. Striking to me is the paragraph headed "hangovers are dangerous." The statement is made that "a hangover effect, produced by alcoholic beverages after the acute intoxication has worn off, may be just as dangerous as the intoxication itself." Symptoms listed include "headache, dizziness, dry mouth, stuffy nose, fatigue, upset stomach, irritability, impaired judgment and increased sensitivity to bright light."

A concluding paragraph is titled "you are in control" and ends with: "The use of alcohol is a significant self-imposed stress factor that should be eliminated from the cockpit. The ability to do so is strictly within the pilot's control." The paper closes with the following general recommendations: 1) Eight hours from 'bottle to throttle,' do not fly while under the influence of alcohol, do not fly while using any drug that may adversely affect safety, 2) a better approach is to wait 24 hours from the last use of alcohol before flying; cold showers, drinking black coffee, and breathing 100 % oxygen cannot speed up the body's elimination of alcohol, 3) consider the adverse effects of a hangover and be aware that your BAC will not necessarily be below legal limits if you follow the eight-hour 'bottle to throttle' guideline, 4) recognize the hazards of combining alcohol consumption and flying, 5) use good judgment---your life and the lives of your passengers are at risk if you drink and fly.

This FAA publication also provided in tabular format some of the effects of various blood alcohol concentrations. They pointed out that the BAC values here overlap because of the wide variation in alcohol tolerance among individuals:

At 0.01-0.05%---average individual appears normal

At 0.03-0.12%---mild euphoria, talkativeness, decreased inhibitions, decreased attention, impaired judgment, increased reaction time

At 0.09-0.25%---emotional instability, loss of critical judgment, impairment of memory and comprehension, decreased sensory response, mild muscular incoordination

At 0.18-0.30%---confusion, dizziness, exaggerated emotions (anger, fear, grief), impaired visual perception, decreased pain sensation, impaired balance, staggering gait, slurred speech, moderate muscular incoordination.

At 0.27-0.40%---apathy, impaired consciousness, stupor, significantly decreased response to stimulation, severe muscular incoordination, inability to stand or walk, vomiting, incontinence of urine and feces.

At 0.35-0.50%---unconsciousness, depressed or abolished reflexes, abnormal body temperature, coma, possible death from respiratory paralysis.

Despite educational efforts by the FAA regulators and the ALPA and individual airline medical departments and management, airmen still fly impaired occasionally. Safety and Policy Analysis International, based in Lafayette, California, published information in 2003 prompted by a rash of then-recent incidents of airline airmen trying to operate aircraft while under the influence of alcohol. While there has never been an airline crash in the U.S. known to be caused by alcohol use, safety concerns are appropriate when airmen violate FAA and airline rules regarding alcohol and flight duty. The FAA now checks a pilot's driving records for DWI convictions when they apply to renew their medical certificate. This trail of FAA data and resulting actions led to 230 revocations/suspensions in year 2000 and 220 in year 2001 with no more recent data available according to that paper. Airlines are required by the FAA to conduct random breath tests of about 10,000 U.S. airline pilots annually. Drug testing began in 1989 and alcohol testing in 1994. Because the failure rate is only 0.1%, regulations permit only 10 % of safety-sensitive airline workers be randomly tested for alcohol annually. The FAA changed policy in January 2003 so that when an airman tests positive for alcohol, the FAA inspector "must revoke both the pilot's medical certificate and the airman's certificate. Both must be valid for a pilot to fly. Pilots must now wait a year and be retested on their flying skills when they complete rehabilitation and regain their medical certificates." The FAA website contains the following statement: "Employers must report to the FAA's Federal Air Surgeon all verified positive drug test results or prohibited alcohol-related conduct for any safety-sensitive employee or applicant who holds a Part 67 Medical Certificate."

The U.S. Department of transportation (DOT) oversees many agencies, one of which is the Federal Aviation Administration (FAA). The DOT employee handbook states the following:

> As a safety-sensitive employee, 1) you must not use or possess alcohol or any illicit drug while assigned to perform safety-sensitive functions or actually performing safety-sensitive functions; 2) you must not report for service or remain on duty if you (a) are under the influence or impaired by alcohol, (b) have a blood alcohol concentration 0.04 or greater [with a blood alcohol concentration of 0.02 to 0.039 some regulations do not permit you to continue working until your next regularly scheduled duty period], (c) have used any illicit drug; 3) you must not use alcohol within four hours [eight hours for flight crew members and flight attendants] of reporting for service or after receiving notice to report; 4) you must not report for duty or remain on duty when using any controlled substance unless used pursuant to the instructions of an authorized medical practitioner; 5) you must not

refuse to submit to any test for alcohol or controlled substances; 6) you must not refuse to submit to any test by adulterating or substituting your specimen.

This directive further clarifies "specimen" collected as urine for drug testing and breath and saliva for alcohol testing. It further states that safety-sensitive employees are subject to drug or alcohol testing in the following situations: 1) pre-employment, 2) reasonable suspicion/cause, 3) random, 4) return to duty, 5) follow-up, 6) post-accident.

The DUI-DWI compliance program (formally labeled DUI-DWI Investigations Program) began in November 1990 by Congressional act. As of year 2001 FAA publication, over four million names of pilots had been submitted to the National Driver Register during that 10-year period. Approximately 100,000 pilots were found on the register with drug or alcohol-related motor vehicle violations, and they were subsequently investigated by the FAA. It should be noted that only about one tenth of one percent of those investigated were airline transport pilots, the bulk being general aviation pilots. Of those 100,000 investigated, over 8,300 enforcement actions were taken and 3,000 pilots lost their medical and airman certificates as a result of those investigations. The FAA added that those 3,000 made up nearly one third of all revocations issued by the FAA.

Although the timing of the Congressional action in this seems more than coincidental to the March 8, 1990, arrest of the drunk Northwest Airlines crew, the FAA points out that the need for increased monitoring became evident in 1988 when the DOT Inspector General's Office conducted an audit of pilots who had records for drug or alcohol-related motor vehicle violations. To ensure compliance with a reporting requirement on the medical certificate application form and to ensure accuracy of FAA records, the FAA gave airmen who had falsified their applications a chance to avoid enforcement action if they volunteered the correct information by a specific date. Thousands of pilots admitted to violating the regulations. Congress tasked the FAA to address the problem of pilots' untruthfulness about their alcohol and drug abuse on applications for medical certificates. The agency began an education campaign to warn pilots that falsification of applications for airmen medical certificates would be caught, investigated and punished. Whereas falsified applications used to be a widespread problem, that is no longer the case since word of the FAA's awareness and action to curb this deceptive pilot behavior was broadcast.

The Chicago Tribune, August 30, 2016, reported on the case of two United Airlines pilots arrested in Scotland for being impaired prior to flying the aircraft to the U.S. While these events are rare, they illustrate the reality that current policy protecting the traveling public from alcoholic airmen is still imperfect. The Tribune article reported only 10 pilots out of 12,480 randomly tested failed the test last year.

It certainly seems reasonable to consider requiring all airline airmen to be tested for alcohol prior to departing with a planeload of passengers as is done in India. That would represent yet another invasion of privacy out of concern for flight safety, but why not in view of the current system imperfection just reviewed? One reason would be that some tests produce false positive results, and the cascade of enforcement actions generated by such false positive tests would be an unacceptable risk.

Although many airline airmen were, like Dad, in excellent health at age 60, that was then the mandatory age for retirement from flight duty. He turned 60 on March 10, 1978, and that also meant an end to his leadership positions in ALPA. The then-President of ALPA, John J. O'Donnell, himself an Eastern Airlines captain, acknowledged Dad's retirement in a congratulatory letter of March 23, 1978, which reads in part:

> The average Association member, including many on Pan Am, will never know of your great devotion to the Association over the years. You were never content to sit passively by and let others do the work. The record indicates that you served as part of the Pan Am pilot delegation that met with founding President Dave Behncke in 1942, a matter involving acquisition of membership by the PAA pilot group. We note that you served several times as Council Chairman in Seattle and always took a deep interest in professional standards questions involving your fellow pilots and became actively a part of the ALPA Human Intervention and Motivation Study when it was initiated some years ago under a grant from the Federal Government. The contributions are only a partial recitation of your many activities and services while a member of ALPA, and were indicative of your recognition of membership responsibility to actively participate in Association affairs. It must now be a great satisfaction and matter of pride to look back over the years and reflect upon the changes, advancements and progress in air transportation, in all of which you have been an active participant and leader.

CHAPTER SIX
HUMAN INTERVENTION & MOTIVATION STUDY (HIMS)

Reference has already been made to human intervention and motivation, but more thorough treatment is now appropriate. I'll begin with historical background because it is fundamental to appreciating the ground-breaking magnitude this represented in commercial aviation.

HIMS originated out of the successful application by ALPA Medical Advisor Dr. Richard Masters to the National Institute on Alcohol Abuse and Alcoholism (NIAAA) for funding a prototype occupational alcoholism program for airline airmen. The premise was that alcohol abuse and alcoholism were no more prevalent among airmen than among other population segments, but all three participants, ALPA, FAA and airline management, agreed that any level of alcohol abuse or alcoholism should be identified and treated.

Originally planned as a five-year study involving three airlines (Continental, Frontier and Braniff), it wound up lasting eight years and including 23 participating airlines. In the HIMS experience, almost 80% of pilots who used the program needed some external work-related pressure to motivate them into treatment. Dad's experience certainly fit that typical characterization.

By 1982 most major U.S. airlines had embraced this program and had developed their own model staffed by HIMS-trained management and ALPA representatives. I have already dealt at length with the development of Pan Am's EAP and Dad's key role throughout that process. Obviously, achieving lasting sobriety for those afflicted with the disease alcoholism enhanced flight safety. Last, but most prominent, the salvage of lives and relationships otherwise destroyed by progressing alcoholism is hard to measure quantitatively. My brothers and our mother can certainly vouch for the successful impact of sobriety in January 1966 when Dad's disease was destroying his marriage and his own physical and mental health.

Sometime in the late 1970's (the document is undated but is in the 1978 section of Dad's files and quotes segments directly from the FAA November 10, 1976, white paper reproduced above), a document was created titled "HIMS SAMPLE OCCUPATIONAL ALCOHOLISM POLICY STATEMENT FOR PILOTS." The document was evidently a 'work in progress' because it is not identical to the final copy included in the final ALPA booklet published March 1982, titled "An Employee Assistance Program for Professional Pilots (An Eight Year Review)."

The booklet came with a cover letter dated August 27, 1982, signed by Dr. Masters, ALPA-HIMS Principle Investigator, and Captain Gilbert Chase, ALPA-HIMS Program Coordinator. I have moved this to the end of the book as Appendix IV. What I have done is *italicized* parts that were removed or revised in the final copy and I have bracketed {**Bold-faced**} added and/or revised versions.

One thing that comes through strongly from viewing both versions is that those running the study learned that there was still a stigma associated with the word "alcoholism" or "alcoholic": for example, they change to "employee assistance policy" instead of "occupational alcoholism policy" and "chemical" instead of "alcohol." Realizing that the original HIMS study had been ongoing for about five years when this detailed policy statement was drafted, it is apparent that a great deal of behind-the-scenes interaction between the ALPA and airlines and FAA must have occurred. Below I have noted sample segments of the eight-year review 33-page brochure published March 1982 by ALPA-HIMS because it provides a blueprint of how one industry succeeded in dealing with the festering sore of concealed alcohol dependency. Dr. Masters wrote the introduction, already quoted in part in the introduction to my manuscript but bearing repeat emphasis here:

> The recognition, management and rehabilitation of alcoholic persons have become, in knowledgeable circles in our society, relatively straightforward and systematized techniques. Much of the success of these measures is due to the integration of the techniques into the work site, thus merging the wherewithal with the motivation. In the early 1970's, no system-wide method of helping airline pilots with alcohol problems or alcoholism had evolved. Some commercial air carriers had recognized the need for occupational alcoholism programs; but few, if any, professional pilots had availed themselves of the meager early programs. The public image problems faced by the pilot's union, the air carriers and the Federal Aviation Administration (FAA) served as a powerful damper to keep the cases hidden. There was a wonderfully synergistic relationship between alcoholism, the supreme manifestation of which is denial, and the fears of pilots, companies and government regulatory agencies manifesting themselves as denial that such problems existed. Hence, the alcoholic pilot denied he had a problem; his fellow pilots, fearing they could cost him his career, denied he had a problem; his supervisors reacted similarly; and the company simply announced they had no alcoholics on their property. The FAA could 'prove' there was no problem, since they almost never got an application from a pilot who proclaimed he was an alcoholic (and if they did, they would efficiently deny certification permanently). So, this mini-society of commercial aviation continued for many years in a conspiracy of silence and denial, unwilling and unable to own the truth that alcoholism was a disease that no more spared pilots than any other segment of society.

But this massive denial did nothing but make the problem worse, often driving the person in need of help underground, where he might get no professional assistance, or an inferior level of assistance. Untreated alcoholism was thus progressing to its often-fatal conclusion.

The Air Line Pilots Association (ALPA) Human Intervention and Motivation Study (HIMS) arose out of a need to face the counterproductive industry attitudes and to bring to the membership a system of help. To launch an industry-wide program, government assistance was seen as necessary, not only for the financial needs, but also to add an element of objectivity and impartiality to the program, so that the FAA, air carriers and the Association could work together toward common goals...

To understand the format of the program described hereinafter, one should know how the Air Line Pilots Association functions. The ALPA was established over 50 years ago to represent pilot groups in the negotiation of working agreements. It now represents about 30,000 professional airline pilots who work for 36 U.S. air carriers. Professionalism and air safety guardianship continue to motivate the actions of the Association while being very successful in achieving its goals in the areas of working conditions and wages. Each air carrier pilot group elects its own officers and negotiates its own contract with the carrier, with technical assistance from the national office of the Association. Local Executive Councils (LEC) at each pilot domicile have three elected officials...a chairman, vice chairman and secretary-treasurer. Domicile LEC's together constitute the Master Executive Council (MEC) for each airline, and this body elects a chairman, vice chairman and secretary-treasurer of the MEC. The MEC Chairman serves as the senior executive officer for representation purposes. The Board of Directors of the Association, composed of all the Master Councils, collectively meets biennially, and is the governing and policy setting body. The President of ALPA, together with First Vice President, Secretary, Treasurer and five Executive Vice Presidents are elected by the Board of Directors and constitute the Executive Committee. The President is the senior executive officer, represents the Association in all instances and carries out the policies and directions of the Board. The Executive Board consists of all MEC Chairmen, meets every six months and governs the Association in the interim period between Board of Directors meetings. In my view, fierce independence of each pilot group is obvious, yet with an overriding element of cohesiveness providing for the strength of the national organization.

Note once again that these excerpts were written in 1982, not now 36 years later. Historical perspectives important to understanding the setting into which ALPA-HIMS was venturing are then addressed:

Prior to 1960, America's millions of alcoholic persons received little or no assistance for the illness at their places of employment. The alcoholic stereotype was an indigent individual whose condition should be treated as criminal or immoral...The few people who recognized alcoholism as an illness often regarded it as self-inflicted. Its victims were seen as irresponsible, rudderless individuals with self-destructive tendencies. The prevailing belief was that treatment could not be effective until the alcoholic 'hit bottom'...When discovered, the alcoholic person was frequently protected from job recrimination...Alcoholism was known to render its victims incapable of having spontaneous insight into the severity of the condition or of requesting assistance...almost no alcoholic person sought assistance without some crisis precipitating the request...precipitating a crisis for the alcoholic person was seen as a method of motivating a change in his behavior. A confrontation in which disciplinary action or loss of livelihood (income) was threatened was a means of motivation...Through this mechanism alcoholic employees were able to receive treatment and subsequently become productive workers...The cooperation of interested parties (both management and union) in successful implementation of such an approach evolved into the concept of occupational alcoholism programs (OAP)...early OAP's had inherent weaknesses...action was initiated only after the late stages of alcoholism were evident....A broader understanding gradually developed in which the legitimate responsibility of a supervisor included not only recognizing signs of the illness but also identifying work performance problems...Administrative procedures allowing a supervisor to document untoward behavior and setting the stage for a constructive confrontation interview were developed. The supervisor and union representative could then refer to professionals capable of diagnosing medical/behavioral problems...In 1974 the National Council on Alcoholism became an advocate for joint union/management OAP's and promoted programs which educated workers regarding symptoms of alcoholism...The OAP's developed policies and procedures to encourage early identification and prevention of alcoholism. The 1970's witnessed maturation of program concepts. In the process of identifying alcoholic persons, related problems surfaced. Programs were broadened to include emotional, family, legal, financial and drug-related problems. The broadened approach became known as Employee Assistance Programs (EAP's). This approach diluted the focus on alcoholism and thereby encouraged more widespread use of services by alcoholics than under OAP's. Employees were urged to seek help...voluntarily; but most...still became identified through 'constructive confrontation'. Vernon E. Johnson...found that through a mechanism he called intervention, the group of individuals expressing concern without coercion often could successfully motivate an affected person to seek help...The Johnson Institute...developed principles of intervention which were based on the belief that delusion or impaired judgment kept an alcoholic...locked into self-destructive patterns keeping him out of touch with reality. It was proposed that an alcoholic was capable of incorporating a useful portion of reality (his drinking behavior) if it were presented in a receivable form. The five principles of intervention include: concern, meaningful people, specific information, realistic alternatives and follow-up. Using these principles, a number of individuals significant to the employee could come together with a feeling of concern to describe specific problem behaviors and offer realistic choices for seeking professional evaluation and assistance with appropriate follow-up. Use of these principles in an intervention format was almost always successful, particularly if a supervisor were involved. This technique could be used on more than one occasion if the initial intervention were unsuccessful or drug-related crises recurred.

The study (HIMS) itself recognized at the outset that the transportation industry was a sensitive work group; that they were resistant to acknowledging the existence of alcoholism in their midst. This was especially true of airlines which harbored particular fear of bad publicity that might result if alcoholic employees, particularly pilots, were discovered. Hence pilots were typically either terminated or retired as soon as their condition became known. At the program's inception, HIMS recognized the following fundamental assumptions:

1. Acceptance of alcoholism as a primary treatable disease

2. Recognition of FAA (Part 67, Federal Aviation regulation) and American Medical Association definition of alcoholism
3. Occupational alcoholism programs are expected to have a higher success rate than non-work related alcoholism programs
4. The intensity of job motivation, characteristic of airline pilots, would be expected to yield a greater recovery rate
5. Total abstinence is essential to successful rehabilitation
6. Alcoholism readily fits the disease prevention model
7. Education can be a factor in changing drinking behavior
8. Early identification of alcoholism is possible and desirable
9. Airline pilot professionalism and the ALPA Code of Ethics promote periodic review of performance
10. Job performance decrement alone is an inadequate basis upon which to identify pilots with alcohol problems
11. Knowledgeable and trained individuals are required to staff the program
12. An open honest approach toward recovery is basic to quality sobriety and is consistent with pertinent Federal Aviation Regulations
13. An alcoholic pilot deserves individual professional attention
14. Unsuccessful repeated efforts at treatment for alcoholism warrant cessation of flying on medical grounds
15. Education of the membership is crucial to the success of the program

The above assumptions served as the basis for the development of the goals and objectives which follow (not ranked in order of priority)

1. To develop, apply and refine a model for early detection, prevention and intervention
2. To educate in sufficient depth to facilitate early identification, prevention and intervention prior to a decrement in job performance due to alcoholism
3. To determine the extent of alcoholism in the pilot group
4. To operate an interim program of assistance
5. To effect a change in the counterproductive restrictions imposed on alcohol abusers by FAA regulations
6. To encourage application of the model through consultation, training and technical assistance
7. To disseminate the model throughout the industry
8. To encourage and train alternative medical and professional resources

HIMS was initially funded for three years with subsequent extensions of two and three years for a total study length of eight years. While the original project was targeted at three comparably sized airlines, 32 of the 36 ALPA member airlines eventually were involved. Privacy was a non-negotiable criterion of HIMS and considered critical to pilot acceptance and to success of the project.

Education was recognized as fundamental to effecting change in behavior. The HIMS project disseminated information to ALPA membership and their families with the primary targets of that information being the social drinker, the early stage problem drinker and the enabler. More specifically, "the educational program centered on changing pilot attitudes toward alcoholism and excessive drinking, decreasing the quantity and frequency of drinking and creating an awareness of project services."

Of particular interest is the fact that airline management and the FAA were also targeted by the project using workshops and information sessions designed to:

> mitigate the counterproductive forces within management and
> FAA which interfered with the identification, rehabilitation and
> return to work of alcoholic pilots. It was recognized that regulatory
> techniques had failed in the area of alcoholism prevention and that
> both management and FAA procedures had fostered reactions of
> fear rather than requests for help. Regular meetings with
> management representatives assisted in this effort by encouraging
> program development and implementation of return to work
> procedures...Regular meetings between HIMS staff and the Federal
> Air Surgeon and his staff focused on the development of
> procedures which would grant alcoholism exemptions in an
> expeditious manner consistent with air safety and the public
> interest. An added benefit of these meetings was the enhancement
> of working relationships between the HIMS staff and the FAA.

HIMS sponsored articles and reports regularly about the project to the entire ALPA membership and to management and other members of the aviation industry. These mailings were consistently followed by an increase in self-referrals and requests for additional information. In fact, the statement is made that "self-referral rates seemed to have a direct relationship to the intensity of the local educational effort." Education empowers!

The Human Intervention Committee (HIC) members were key players in the conduct of the project. These were made up of at least one captain, one first officer and one second officer with the expectation that they be "interested in the project, willing to serve approximately three years and be able to work cooperatively with management. Personal experience with alcoholism is not a prerequisite for membership." Characteristics of committee members that fostered more effective committee functioning included 1) empathy and sensitivity to human needs, 2) non-judgmental attitudes toward people with medical/behavioral problems (including alcoholism), 3) understanding and appreciation for the various roles and functions required in an EAP, 4) understanding of union activities and an ability to work within the professional ethics of the ALPA, 5) the ability to gain and preserve the respect of peers, 6) the ability to keep confidences and to respect confidential information, 7) recovering alcoholics who have a minimum of two years of total abstinence and have disclosed their own illness to the FAA. By the eight-year end of the project, sixteen airlines representing 90 % of ALPA membership had developed a formal EAP. Cost-benefit analysis by HIMS on a sampling of cases indicated that "an airline could conservatively expect a $9.00 return for every $1.00 invested in a professionally managed EAP for pilots."

Another measure of HIMS success can be seen in the durability of total abstinence-sobriety which is what the FAA and HIMS require for problem alcoholics. Of HIMS-facilitated FAA exemptions for alcoholism over the eight years of the project, 20% relapsed. Of those who returned to drinking, 35% underwent further treatment with good response and granting of a second exemption for an overall long-term recovery rate of 85% (Recovery is here defined as total abstinence from any alcoholic beverages).

The eight-year HIMS project report concluded, in part, as follows:

> By primarily emphasizing peer identification and secondarily, supervisory identification, many pilots have received assistance who would not otherwise have been reached. Peers have become involved voluntarily and the ALPA has provided the structure for effective peer review and intervention where coercion alone was not a realistic motivator. In the future, three critical factors require resolution in order for airlines to maintain effective pilot programs. First, management must recognize the legitimacy of a program designed specifically for pilots which incorporates the HIMS model into overall company practices. Second, airline management must recognize that, although costs are incurred in administering the program, maximum effectiveness will be achieved only by continuing to involve company and ALPA representatives equally in program decisions. The cost effectiveness of this approach has been pointed out. Third, it is recommended that each MEC continue its close participation throughout the development and refinement of programs.

> The airline which initially had the poorest labor/management relationship was the first to formalize a program. This was the result of a continuing commitment by the MEC to develop the

program. It would appear that strong comprehensive programs can develop even within carriers where labor/management relations are strained...The involvement of recovering alcoholic persons was minimal at first but increased over time. Concurrently, the program was in transition from an only alcoholism to an employee assistance concept. Participation by recovering alcoholic individuals helped to develop enthusiasm and commitment to the EAP concept, while at the same time maintaining an alcoholism emphasis. It is recommended that the ALPA and management committees should have an equal ratio of recovering alcoholic and non-alcoholic members in an effort to maintain the strength of the program, yet minimize a specific program stereotype.

A cautionary statement needs emphasis: the HIMS-trained volunteers are not diagnosticians but rather identifiers of problems and/or drinking behavior. "Intervention is not predicated upon a union representative or supervisory diagnosis."

Further caution was emphasized that inappropriate labeling of a pilot, as alcoholic when he is not, must be avoided because of the negative effects on his FAA certification. "Therefore, the HIMS recommends careful selection of independent diagnostic assessment resources." HIMS recommended Alcoholics Anonymous as a support system and a useful part of aftercare and pointed out that "the FAA endorsed active participation in A.A., yet required periodic review within a clinical setting. Mandated aftercare continues for a minimum of 24 months based on an FAA assumption that at the end of that period the recovering alcoholic should have no greater risk of returning to drinking than his initial risk of becoming an alcoholic."

In conclusion, this project report noted that although the original target population had been the 30,000 pilots, the concept of EAP's in the airline industry had grown those eight years to encompass the entire 300,000 employee industry...and ALPA had been the catalyst for that spread to the industry as a whole.

The current HIMS website continues this theme by stating: "HIMS is specific to commercial pilots and coordinates the identification, treatment and return to the cockpit of impaired aviators. It is an industry-wide effort in which companies, pilot unions, and FAA work together to preserve careers and further air safety." While I'm no English major, the first sentence might be better stated as follows: HIMS is specific to commercial pilots and coordinates the identification of impaired pilots, their treatment and their return to flight status. Best not to even hint at a "cockpit of impaired aviators" as a HIMS goal! I urge readers to view the 14-minute video posted on the HIMS homepage (access via webpage at www.himsprogram.com). That is especially important for those airmen who have an alcohol problem and for family and friends of those airmen suspected of having an alcohol problem. In that video, you will meet now-sober alcoholic pilots whose willingness to share their own struggles with booze testify to the effectiveness of the HIMS program at salvaging careers and restoring health. The website provides the following mission statement:

> The purpose of the HIMS program is to effectively treat the disease of chemical dependency in pilot populations in order to save lives and careers while enhancing flight safety. The HIMS concept is based on a cooperative and mutually supportive relationship between pilots, their management, and the FAA. Trained managers and peer pilots interact to identify and, in many cases, conduct an intervention to direct the troubled individual to a substance abuse professional for a diagnostic evaluation. If deemed medically necessary, treatment is then initiated. Following successful treatment and comprehensive continuing care, the pilot is eligible to seek FAA medical re-certification.

> The FAA requires the pilot to be further evaluated by a specially trained FAA Aviation Medical Examiner (AME) who then acts as the Independent Medical Sponsor (IMS) to coordinate the FAA re-certification process. The medical sponsor provides oversight of the pilot's continuing care. This care includes a monthly interview by a trained flight manager and by a pilot peer committee member, as well as periodic follow-up observations. Because of the relapse potential of chemical dependency, the monitoring will typically continue for several years after the pilot resumes his duties. The HIMS program is designed to ensure the pilot maintains total abstinence and to protect flight safety.

What follows now is taken directly from the HIMS website. It provides excellent background into Employee Assistance Programs (EAP) as they relate to airline airmen:

> Understanding the Employee Assistance Program (EAP) concept requires an awareness of the history of occupational alcoholism programming going back to the early 1940's. The appearance of industrial alcoholism programs in the early 1940's as an outgrowth of a) the successful recoveries effected through Alcoholics Anonymous, founded in 1935, and b) the founding in 1940 of the Section on Alcohol Studies, Laboratory of Applied Physiology at Yale University. Beginning in the mid-1940's, tentative programs began to evolve within a handful of major industrial firms; the alcoholism movement had also been gaining strength and allies. The basic idea back then was that supervisors could be trained in the symptomatology of alcoholism and look for

these symptoms among their subordinates. The most common symptoms mentioned were blood-shot eyes, trembling hands and the smell of alcohol on the breath. The image of the alcoholic employee was not far from the Skid-Road stereotype. The employees identified in these early programs were late alcoholics whose problems were so overt they were obvious to virtually everyone.

Over the years some major problems developed with this approach. To begin with, first line supervisors did the identification and diagnosis and as a result no one above his/her level received help. Consequently, the only people identified were non-supervisory employees even though all evidence indicated that alcoholism affects every occupational and professional level. Furthermore, expecting a supervisor to make medically-related diagnoses resulted in legal problems for the supervisor. A second major problem was that alcoholics were skillful at diverting attention away from their real problem---masters at employing the 'Con Game.' With relative ease, the employee convinced the supervisor that the 'real problem' was a nagging or spendthrift spouse, an unmanageable child, a physical ailment, money problems, or plain bad luck. Matching a supervisor with a practicing alcoholic was simply no contest---the supervisor lost nearly every time. Termination or early retirement at a reduced income usually became the solution. Everyone lost. Finally, because of the stigma associated with alcoholism, supervisors wanted to be certain beyond a reasonable doubt that alcoholism really was the problem. Fearing the embarrassment of misidentification, the supervisor waited until the employee evidenced several obvious chronic stage symptoms. In 1972, the Occupational Programs Branch of the NIAAA surveyed existing employer programs countrywide. Out of approximately three hundred companies with a written policy, it was found that only a fraction were working with an acceptable degree of success. Most had started out fast because it was relatively easy to identify chronic or terminal stage alcoholics. After an initial surge, however, many programs slowed and penetration of the population at risk was low. However, there were some distinct elements common to the successful programs and it is from these that the 'troubled employee' concept had its genesis and from which the Employee Assistance concept had its genesis.

The object of these early EAP's was to avoid the problems experienced in supervisor-diagnosed alcoholism programs while successfully identifying and referring those who needed help. A variety of other problems, such as marital, financial, physical, psychological, legal, social, vocational misplacement and job boredom were found to also cause unacceptable job performance. Under the EAP umbrella all troubled employees were offered assistance and supervisors were trained to monitor job performance and refer when normal progressive discipline failed to correct the behavior. The effectiveness of this approach rested in three areas: (1) a reduced stigma to EAP, (2) earlier identification, and (3) the fact that the employer controlled the paycheck---in the case of addicted employees, the money needed to keep drinking and using drugs. Supervisors/managers were able to successfully intervene with resistant and troubled employees through the threat of job loss. One of the 1974 initiatives of the NIAAA was funding of the HIMS. It was apparent to the Occupational Programs Branch that traditional intervention methods---referral by supervisors as a result of an employee's deteriorating performance---did not work well for top executives, professionals, or safety-sensitive positions like airline pilots. Executives and professionals had been virtually impossible for EAP's to reach because slippages in work performance were harder to detect and there were elaborate cover-ups by peers. By that time, groups such as doctors, lawyers and nurses were beginning to address peer-referral groups, but special EAP's for professionals and executives were virtually non-existent. Pilots have a high degree of autonomy, strong denial mechanisms, and a great fear of admitting that they may have a substance abuse or emotional problem. By the early 1970's, the art of identifying and treating employed alcoholics was progressing through a technique known as 'constructive confrontation.' While these confrontations were being applied with considerable success, even among other airline workgroups, little help was available for the employed pilot. Strict enforcement of regulations by the FAA continued to create an insurmountable obstacle for the afflicted pilot. Fellow pilots were reluctant to intervene (confront) for fear of threatening a colleague's livelihood. In 1974 the Air Line Pilots Association (ALPA) took the initiative through a grant from the National Institute of Alcohol Abuse and Alcoholism (NIAAA). They, in cooperation with the FAA and airline management, developed a prototype occupational alcoholism program for pilots. The project was called the Human Intervention and Motivation Study (HIMS).

The HIMS Program website provides detailed guidelines for airlines desiring to create their own EAP. An important caution: "Some of the people most committed to developing an EAP are recovering chemically dependent pilots. The caveat here is that they be 'well grounded' in their sobriety. From experience, it is suggested that they wait until all FAA monitoring ceases before becoming a member of the peer team." Knowledge is power and knowing about the accessibility of this website, www.himsprogram.com, is key AFTER recognizing you or some airman you care about has a problem. But the first step is recognizing there is a problem. Under the "Get Help Now" website sub-head is "pilot referral info" where 40 airlines are listed together with the name of that company's HIMS representative, phone number and e-mail address. Another confidential resource is the website www.alpa.org for ALPA members where you are advised to log in and refer to your airline's HIMS committee roster for contact information. Finally, HIMS website advises contacting an expert aeromedical physician at Aviation Medicine Advisory Service (720)857-6117, Monday through Friday, 8:30 AM-4:00 PM Mountain Time. Whichever of these three resources you choose to contact, the website reminds you, **"It's important to actively seek help for yourself or someone you care about."**

Now that we've examined in detail the HIMS from ALPA's viewpoint, it is appropriate to get the FAA's point of view. In October 1985, a report titled "Alcohol Rehabilitation of Airline Pilots" was released by authors Russell and Davis of the FAA Civil Aeromedical Institute, part of the Office of Aviation Medicine within the Federal Aviation Administration. They concluded that the coordinated efforts of the FAA, the ALPA and several airlines initiated in 1976 aimed at medical certification of rehabilitated alcoholic pilots had a "surprising rate of success." There was an 85% success rate involving over 500 airline pilots since 1976. Importantly, they concluded that when pilots relapsed and were taken off flight duty and recycled through the program, aviation safety was not compromised. Some general features of most of the pilot group included being early or middle stage alcoholics, with few arrests or run-ins with the law, with high occupational stability and high occupational achievement, were an older age at diagnosis, and married. These are features which have been associated with successful outcomes in treatment of alcoholism.

Twenty-three percent of these alcoholic pilots were self-referred for treatment while 60% were referred by ALPA and/or the employer airline. Seventeen percent were referred by families or other sources such as counseling centers and the courts. Pilots were required to go through an approved inpatient treatment program followed by outpatient aftercare with psychiatric and psychological evaluations performed one to three months after treatment. Each pilot was required to have a medical monitor (airline medical director, the ALPA medical advisor or an aviation medical examiner experienced in alcohol treatment and counseling) who was responsible for the subsequent 24-month monitoring period. This was a staged progressive process with a "special issuance" granted in 80% of the cases within one year of treatment. Monitoring was still rigorous with monthly reports required from the airline flight operations supervisor and an ALPA representative attesting to the individual's sobriety. Quarterly reports from the aftercare program and annual or semiannual psychiatric evaluations were also required. After 24 months the medical monitor could petition the Federal Air Surgeon to remove the monitoring requirement although monitoring could continue if the psychiatrist or aftercare counselor or medical monitor felt the pilot had not yet achieved stable sobriety.

This FAA report made an interesting observation regarding alcoholism prevalence among airline pilots. Contemporary data on railroad engineers and conductors show 23% are problem drinkers, and occupational factors common to railroad engineers and pilots are irregular working hours and long layovers away from home. No actual prevalence data was cited for airline pilots however. The supportive social network of friends, family and coworkers needed to successfully recover from alcoholism has often been effectively destroyed by the time alcoholism is diagnosed. The 24 months of monthly monitoring help in restoring a supportive network through building participation in aftercare, Birds of a Feather (B.O.A.F.) and Alcoholics Anonymous (A.A.) which provide social environments focused on non-drinking activities. Seventy-nine percent of the pilot group had not had a relapse since receiving "special issuance" and 6% more achieved certification after one or two relapses. Of note, 9% relapsed and did not reapply, 1% were terminated for failure to comply with monitoring requirements and 5% were terminated for other medical complications, accounting for the 15% failure to be medically certified rate. It is interesting that those pilots with military flight history were more likely to relapse the greater their military flight time. Family participation both in the inpatient treatment phase and in aftercare (i.e. Alanon, Alateen, family or group therapy) correlated with higher success rate. An interesting observation from this group was that pilots who have "an alcoholic family member may find it easier to admit their own alcoholism and consequently have a more favorable treatment outcome." Relapse was predictably more likely in those under 40 years of age. This report's concluding paragraph sentence deserves quoting: "A government regulatory agency (FAA), a large union (ALPA), and the management of several airline companies have demonstrated the ability of sometimes opposing forces to work together to combat a major public health problem and enhance air safety."

Since the advent of HIMS-ALPA in 1974, approximately 6,500 pilots, nearly 150 per year, have gone through rehabilitation and regained their medical certificates. Random drug and alcohol testing, mandated and carried out by the FAA, is now a reality. For example, 2015 data shows ten who were randomly tested out of 12,480 pilots had blood alcohol concentrations of greater than 0.04 mg percent. For 2014 and 2013, random testing failures amounted to thirteen and five respectively. Overall about one in ten "safety sensitive employees" in the airline industry are randomly tested for alcohol annually. The FAA considers safety sensitive to include flight crew members, flight attendants, aircraft or ground dispatchers, aircraft maintenance personnel, aviation security or screening personnel and air-traffic controllers.

There is good reason to challenge the FAA's choice of 0.04 mg percent as the threshold for test failure. From my medical field comes excellent relevant information published in the esteemed New England Journal of Medicine, August 16, 1990, issue titled, "Drinking and Flying---The Problem of Alcohol Use by Pilots," authored by Modell and Mountz. The data I here recount is still pertinent despite being nearly three decades old. An especially alarming fact is the reality that pilot flight performance can be impaired many hours after consuming alcohol, and at a time when BAC has fallen to zero. Alcohol-induced changes in eye movement termed nystagmic response to Coriolis acceleration can persist up to 34 hours after ingesting three to seven standard alcoholic drinks. This positional alcohol nystagmus occurs then whenever the head is tilted relative to a plane of rotation. The result is false perceptions of position and movement similar to those encountered during flight--- disturbance in visual and vestibular systems critical to flight performance.

Another cited study involved young healthy Navy pilots flying large multi-engine aircraft. Their flight performance was studied in a land-based flight simulator 14 hours after their last drink when measured BAC had fallen to zero after ingesting 4.5 to 6.5 standard alcoholic drinks, and then compared to their performance during the no-alcohol control test. Decreases in precision and accuracy on all variables tested were found associated with heavy drinking the night before testing. Variables adversely impacted included take-off heading, landing heading, instrument-landing localizer and glide slope deviation, yaw (aircraft rotation in any one of three dimensions) on take-off, and yaw on landing. Of particular note was the fact that pilots were unable to accurately judge their own degree of flight impairment the morning after ingesting that alcohol despite undetectable BAC. This scholarly review by the University of Michigan researchers recommended the allowable BAC be reduced from 0.04 to zero, and the "bottle-to-throttle" rule increased from 8 hours to at least 12 hours. Neither of these recommendations has been enacted over the intervening 27 years. So much for science and safety! Fortunately, many airlines (but not the FAA) have tightened the "bottle-to-throttle" from 8 up to 12 hours, but the BAC allowable limit is still the same as NTSB's commercial trucker allowable of 0.04 for reasons entirely obscure to me. One clear improvement is the requirement for aviators to report DUI's, within 60 days of their occurrence, to the FAA. Additionally, these authors advised that a revised Federal Aviation Regulation 91.17 include a preamble explicitly stating the following:

1. Impairment of a pilot's performance sufficient to jeopardize the safety of a flight can occur after consumption of a single alcoholic drink a few hours before flight.

2. Such impairment can also persist for up to 24 hours after the consumption of five or more standard alcoholic drinks or in the presence of any aftereffects of drinking.

3. For each standard alcoholic drink consumed, two or more hours may be required for it to be metabolized and eliminated sufficiently to reduce blood alcohol concentrations to undetectable levels. A standard alcoholic drink is defined as approximately 360 ml of beer, 150 ml of wine, or 44 ml of liquor; all are equally detrimental to pilot performance.

I need to emphasize a key point: the HIMS program is not a policing action. Rather, it should be viewed as a vital helping resource toward improved pilot health and public safety. Hence, getting an alcohol dependent pilot into treatment sooner rather than later may be the most helpful thing a caring peer can do for his or her fellow pilot. Helping an alcoholic pilot get needed help with their disease before they have violated FAA regulations or company policy regarding alcohol can be the most effective way to help preserve their aviation career.

Lyle Prouse sent me the following personal communication which is relevant as I end the chapter on the ALPA-HIMS program:

Alcoholism is marked by severe mental and emotional denial of the disease itself, and the worse one gets, the more convinced they are it will get better, and I can personally attest to this. In 1990, I became the first commercial airline pilot ever arrested, tried, convicted, and sentenced to federal prison for having flown a commercial airliner under the influence of alcohol. Everyone, including myself, was absolutely convinced and certain I would never fly again. I was terminated, stripped of all my licenses, went broke, and was sent to federal prison. The judge put sanctions on me that guaranteed I would never fly again, and though I was destroyed and devastated by it all, I accepted all of this as fair and appropriate. I entered treatment the day after my arrest, on March 9, 1990, and have been sober ever since.

Had it not been for the fact that alcoholism is now recognized as a treatable and recoverable disease, and had it not been for the HIMS regimen I was able to comply with, my fate would have been sealed---and rightly so. As it was, I retired as a 747 captain for the same airline I so horribly and egregiously shamed, embarrassed, and disgraced, and, later, my trial judge would lead the way to a Presidential Pardon for me. Captain Buckingham's courageous leadership, and that of all other parties involved, made it possible for me to do the impossible. I am retired now but will remain forever grateful to those who paved the way for me and countless others.

The HIMS program has evolved into an extremely sophisticated process requiring, among many other things, complex and sophisticated testing for mental, emotional, and neurological damage as well as long term monitoring (three years), frequent random testing at all hours day and night, weekly peer monitoring, and hands-on involvement with airline management, Chief Pilots, EAP (Employee Assistance Program), and HR personnel. Without the courage of pilots like Captain Buckingham, Dr. Masters, and those dauntless FAA leaders, none of this could have occurred. The safety of American aviation cannot be over-exaggerated as a result of those early pioneers and the risks they took to engage the problem and develop this program.

For those desiring more detail on intervention, treatment, aftercare and monitoring as well as pilot referral contacts for 40 airlines, please turn to appendix I.

CHAPTER SEVEN
BIRDS OF A FEATHER (BOAF) & OTHER AFTERCARE
"We too did some good social drinking. Then the day arrived when liquor
was no longer a social lubricant but an absolute necessity. We who were
then possessed with shakes, cold sweats and jitters flocked together and
did a fine job of drying up."

According to the document saved among Dad's papers, the above three sentences
headed the one-page flyer of the BOAF organization. As Dad was dying of lung
cancer in 1994, he was asked how he would most desire to be remembered. Without
hesitation, he declared, "as an airman and co-founder of BOAF." Mind you, don't
think for a minute that he wasn't profoundly thankful for and to his devoted wife of
54 years and his three sons. But he remained steadfast in his acknowledgement that
A.A. saved him for 28 years of sobriety as a recovered alcoholic. He saved a one-page
document from a physician Medical Director of an Alcoholism Recovery Unit titled
"FOR THE PHYSICIAN—THE RECOVERY PROCESS FROM ALCOHOLISM—12 GUIDING
PRINCIPLES." These are so important I list them here:

1. In alcoholism and for the alcoholic, medicine and psychiatry offer
    nothing that in and of itself is curative. It is necessary we
    recognize and accept this.

2. There is a specific and complete method of recovery in the twelve
    suggested steps of recovery of Alcoholics Anonymous.

3. The alcoholic begins the recovery by acknowledging his addiction,
    his powerlessness over alcohol, and the unmanageability of his
    life.

4. The alcoholic cannot stop drinking permanently without
    undergoing a profound personality change in the nature of a
    transformation.

5. This change is an internal process, the answer within oneself, and
    is not provided by outside means or sources. These may assist in
    the process and are often essential.

6. The acknowledgement of a power greater than one's own ego, and
    a surrender to that is fundamental. This higher power guides the
    alcoholic in the ongoing recovery process.

7. The alcoholic begins to let go of the old life, the one that didn't work, and in which drinking was his recourse until it, too, didn't work---and he became alcoholic.

8. The alcoholic comes to discover a new way of living wherein the quality of his life is not determined by events, conditions or circumstances, but by his attitudes about those events, conditions and circumstances, no matter what.

9. This shift from being the effect (victim) of those conditions to being the cause of one's own experience of living is in the nature of a transformation, a spiritual awakening or enlightenment.

10. Without this awakening or transformation, the quality of sobriety is diminished, limited, and robbed of the wellbeing and joy of living, which are its real goal.

11. The family of the alcoholic is also sick and will use these same Twelve Steps of Recovery. The recovery process of the alcoholic manifests in its most impressive form when alcoholism is treated in this way as a family disease.

12. Persons regarded as treaters---doctors, counselors, nurses---also join the recovery process, and using these same principles experience a transformation. The process in the alcoholic and co-alcoholic is limitless and life becomes a series of endless possibilities instead of endless problems.

Ref: Richard Carlson, M.D., Alcoholism Recovery Unit...location and date unknown
While there is overlap between the list above, and the 12-step program of A.A. listed below, theirs is somewhat different and merits noting:

1. We admitted we were powerless over alcohol---that our lives had become unmanageable.

2. Came to believe that a Power greater than ourselves could restore us to sanity.

3. Made a decision to turn our will and our lives over to the care of God as we understood Him.

4. Made a searching and fearless moral inventory of ourselves.

5. Admitted to God, to ourselves, and to another human being the exact nature of our wrongs.
6. We're entirely ready to have God remove all these defects of character.
7. Humbly asked Him to remove our shortcomings.
8. Made a list of all persons we had harmed, and became willing to make amends to them all.
9. Made direct amends to such people wherever possible, except when to do so would injure them or others.
10. Continued to take personal inventory and when we were wrong promptly admitted it.
11. Sought through prayer and meditation to improve our conscious contact with God, as we understood Him, praying only for knowledge of His will for us and the power to carry that out.
12. Having had a spiritual awakening as the result of these Steps, we tried to carry this message to alcoholics, and to practice these principles in all our affairs.

Ref: Hazelden Betty Ford

For Dad, step 12 was key to his recovery. Nearly one year to the day since achieving lasting sobriety, he penned a hand-written letter to his best friend and fellow senior Pan Am pilot, Captain Lyman ("Mike") Watt. Dad was following the directive to "carry this message to alcoholics." (Permission to name Mike was given by his eldest surviving adult child.) Dad's missive of January 9, 1967, reads:

I must say that there must be something in this ESP business. Call it premonition or a kindred spirit sort of thing, but I've had the feeling for the past couple of weeks that all was not well with my old buddy. Guess the Lord must have plans for you. You must know that damn few people live through such an anaphylactic shock as you experienced from the combination of shots you were given. I am certainly glad to hear that your recovery will be complete and soon.

I'm going to give you some unsolicited advice but before I do, I'm going to relate to you what following this advice did for me. A little more than a year ago I had reached the complete end of my tether. A series of disappointments, frustrations and disillusionments had brought me to the point. The only way I could face life was to be at least half juiced, and even then I had nothing but a complete loathing for myself. I had practically ruined my health, had no self-respect and no one understood (or so I thought). On two occasions I attempted to take my own life, fortunately (depending on one's point of view) neither was successful. To make a long messy story short, my life was a complete shambles. Everything I had strived for was going down the drain, and I was powerless to help it. I just couldn't fathom a life without alcohol.

Savory, the chief, contacted A.A. for me and even then for a period of a couple of months I still fought sobriety. However, the philosophy of A.A. finally rubbed off onto me and I woke up sober one morning free from the desire to drink. It still took a couple of months for my thinking to get back to the normal thoughts I'd missed for years. I've accomplished more in the past twelve months than I had in the previous twelve years. Now that I have my head back and am able to think properly, I can associate alcohol with everything bad that ever happened to me.

We pilots are a strange breed, Mike. We have a feeling that we are accountable only to ourselves and can find whatever help we need within ourselves, a self-sufficient island so to speak. Such is nothing further from the truth. Give yourself a break and turn your life over to the will of God. Take each day as it comes and live for that day alone. Consider this: 'God grant me the serenity to accept the things I cannot change, the courage to change the things I can, and the wisdom to know the difference.' I hope you don't mistake the content of this letter. I just hope it spares you a measure of the misery I know is waiting for you if you don't act now.

Sincerely, Buck

Mike's son, who sent me this 40-year-old letter, commented, "I have to believe it was a crucial component in my Dad deciding to sort himself out and give up drinking. Buck was certainly his best friend, and it is likely only a best friend could weigh in with this kind of counsel and get away with it, especially given my Dad's stubbornness. My Dad did develop (as did yours) the reformed drunk's zeal to 'cure' other people, and both of our Dads felt how threatened the whole industry was by this epidemic disease." What a tribute to the import and impact of a true friend! We all would do well to take note and act on behalf of others diseased when the opportunity presents itself in the living of our lives.

Credit is given to Dad for speaking at a November 1972 ALPA Board of Directors meeting about the need to keep pilot's jobs after they are in recovery from treatment for alcohol abuse and alcoholism. Dad was one of three recovered alcoholic men who met in 1975 to discuss the need for an A.A. meeting for airmen only. BOAF held its first meeting on December 5, 1975. About that time, Dad let the FAA know he was a recovering alcoholic, but their response was that it was self-diagnosis and they would have nothing to do with it. Their early meetings were criticized by some other A.A. groups who accused BOAF of discriminating against non-flight individuals.

Apparently, BOAF learned to combat such assertions of discrimination by referring to their gathering as a "meeting" rather than a "group." The California BOAF "nest" was formed a year later, and Dr. Joseph Pursch was made an honorary "Bird."

I had the privilege of attending one of those early 1970's Seattle BOAF meetings at which Dr. Pursch was the invited guest speaker. I'll never forget walking into the banquet room and, as Dad was introducing me to him, I noted with horror the prominently displayed beverage bottles gracing the center of each round table. My immediate reaction was: what are champagne bottles doing at an A.A.-type function?

I'm sure both Dad and Dr. Pursch got a charge out of my alarmed distracted state; those "champagne" bottles were actually Martinelli's apple cider which I had never seen before. Dr. Pursch was a nationally recognized leader in the field of alcohol and drug abuse who wrote the book *Dear Doc* in 1983 and was the treating physician for many famous recovering alcoholics.

The Birds of a Feather International website features a home page defining BOAF as "a worldwide network of meetings based on the program of Alcoholics Anonymous." Furthermore, it was "established for pilots and cockpit crew members active or inactive in private, commercial or military aviation. We provide A.A. meetings worldwide, a yearly convention, a newsletter and this website for pilots and cockpit crew members in recovery."

Under heading, "Our Singleness of Purpose," it reads:

> Birds of a Feather was formed in response to the need for meeting places for pilots and cockpit crew members where the subject of addiction to alcohol might be discussed with impunity and anonymity. The cultural bias concerning this subject has prevented many in the past from seeking advice. Our concern is recovery from alcoholism. We have no loyalties to any company, government institution, medical facility, union, employee assistance plan, treatment center or specific recovery program. BOAF has contributed immeasurably to our recovery and the spirit of passing this philosophy on to others who also might benefit is the reason for Birds of a Feather.

Posted on the second page of BOAF website is an excerpt from Dad's May 6, 1978 address at the Alcohol Awareness Hour at Eisenhower Medical Center:

> About BOAF: A clinical diagnosis of alcoholism or a history of an excessive drinking habit disqualifies an aviator from holding the FAA medical certificate which permits him to work as an airman. Thus an aviator having a problem with alcohol whose

condition became known was automatically grounded. BOAF was formed in 1975 to assist troubled airmen to sobriety, thereby saving lives and careers. It was formed by three recovered pilots and two non-pilot airmen in the Pacific Northwest. In 1976 the Federal Air Surgeon, H. L. Reighard, a very perceptive and realistic practitioner, believed that air safety is to be enhanced by assisting airmen to recovery rather than having them remain in the closet along with their booze. BOAF has done exactly as the founders had hoped: assisting airmen toward sobriety.

Currently, forty-three "nests" are listed with regular meeting schedules including overseas sites as distant as Hong Kong and the Netherlands. Twelve other "nests" are listed but meet on an irregular basis. Eighty-two "solo birds" have agreed to allow their listing as such in locations where no regularly meeting "nest" exists. All of this is also provided on their website. It is clear from this that the sites and their availability are not intended to be exclusive but rather to welcome those airmen needing and desiring ongoing fellowship and support. That is certainly consistent with Dad's founding vision.

The label, Alcohol Awareness Hour, originated Nov. 13, 1976, at the Rancho Mirage location of Eisenhower medical Center. It was co-founded by Dr. Joseph Cruse, then president of the Medical Center staff, and retired radio legend Del Sharbutt and his wife, singer Meri Bell...all prominent people in long-term recovery themselves. Dad's presentation in 1978 centered on Birds of a Feather, and he returned for a couple years more as speaker there, and probably would have done so longer if his youngest son (my brother, Mike Buckingham) had not been the victim of a drunk driver on April 12, 1981. As if Mike's seven-month stay in Harborview's famed Burn Center wasn't enough of an adjustment for the entire family, Dad himself cheated death June 7, 1982, when an incompetent anesthesiologist caused complications of elective orthopedic surgery with permanent sequelae. I'll address that later. Meanwhile know that Dad's 1978 talk generated the following acknowledgement from Del and Meri Bel Sharbutt quoted in part below:

> Dear Buck:
> Those of us working for more professional and public awareness of alcohol use and abuse owe a deep debt of gratitude to you for the Birds of a Feather participation in our program at Eisenhower on May 6th. You, Joan, Chuck and our local buddy Joe made a powerful contribution, and we thank you. You know what we must do? All of you must come back and do it all over again next year.

The Betty Ford Center adopted this Saturday morning educational and inspirational program in 1982 which continues today as the Awareness Hour. Dad had been summoned by Betty Ford's doctor, Dr. Joseph Pursch, to participate in former First Lady Betty Ford's intervention in 1978. He initiated in Seattle an Alcohol Awareness Hour on Saturday mornings at Seattle University together with noted addiction expert, Father James Royce. I attended one session, probably in 1982, where I heard something I needed to hear from Sharon Wegscheider on adult children of an alcoholic. Until that day I had simply 'cruised along' oblivious to the reality that my being had been impacted by living through Dad's alcoholism during my development years of childhood. Now Mrs. Wegscheider-Cruse, she herself grew up with an alcoholic father who drank himself to death. She trained as a substance abuse counselor and joined Al-anon, an organization designed for family and friends of alcoholics, to deal better with residua of her father's alcoholism and its effect on her. She became convinced that "it was not enough to work with the alcoholic. We had to work with the family too."

The first Adult Children of Alcoholics (ACA) meeting began in the mid-1970's and gave birth to what was labeled "The Laundry List," characteristics that seem common to those raised in an alcoholic household. Between we three brothers, several of the following list fit but some do not: 1) we became isolated and afraid of people and authority figures 2) we became approval seekers and lost our identity in the process 3) we are frightened by angry people and any personal criticism 4) we either become alcoholics or marry them or both or find another compulsive personality such as a workaholic to fulfill our sick abandonment needs 5) we live life from the viewpoint of victims and are attracted by that weakness in our love and friendship relationships, 6) we have an overdeveloped sense of responsibility and it is easier for us to be concerned with others rather than ourselves...this enables us not to look too closely at our own faults 7) we get guilt feelings when we stand up for ourselves instead of giving in to others 8) we become addicted to excitement 9) we confuse love with pity and tend to "love" people who we can "pity" and "rescue" 10) we have stuffed our feelings from our traumatic childhoods and have lost the ability to feel or express our feelings because it hurts so much (denial) 11) we judge ourselves harshly and have a very low sense of self-esteem 12) we are dependent personalities who are terrified of abandonment and will do anything to hold on to a relationship in order not to experience painful abandonment feelings which we received from living with sick people who were never there emotionally for us 13) alcoholism is a family disease and we became para-alcoholics and took on the characteristics of the disease even though we did not pick up the drink 14) para-alcoholics are reactors rather than actors.

I find another listing of features of we adult children more in keeping with my family upbringing: 1) guess at what normal is 2) have difficulty in following a project through from beginning to end 3) lie when it would be just as easy to tell the truth 4) judge themselves without mercy 5) have difficulty having fun 6) take themselves very seriously 7) have difficulty with intimate relationships 8) overreact to changes over which they have no control 9) constantly seek approval and affirmation 10) feel that they are different from other people 11) are either super responsible or super irresponsible 12) are extremely loyal even in the face of evidence that loyalty is undeserved 13) tend to lock themselves into a course of action without giving serious consideration to alternative behaviors or possible consequences.

I personally find Mrs. Wegscheider-Cruse's labeling of family roles, as they relate to the alcoholic member, more helpful in a practical sense than the "laundry list." Her 1981 book, *Another Chance*, spells these out in detail, and I will endeavor here to apply them to my own family. She makes the important observation that in an alcoholic family, the individual family member gets "trapped into one role, and his personal potentials are gradually deformed to fit its demands. He slowly becomes the role." Furthermore, "switching roles for any reason is not really common. Each role grows out of its own kind of pain, has its own symptoms, offers its own payoffs for both the individual and the family, and ultimately exacts its own price."

Dad was of course the alcoholic (the *dependent*). The spouse is usually the *enabler* and, indeed, Mother filled that role. "An enabling wife often acts out of a sincere, if misguided, sense of love and loyalty." If she harbored fear over the possible imagined consequences of Dad's alcoholic behavior, she certainly did not communicate that to us three boys. I suppose she took steps to discourage his drinking those last several worst years of his disease, but other than emptying the contents of booze bottles she'd find hidden here and there throughout their home I'm not aware of other actions taken by her. Unknowingly, her "super-responsible posture" was "actually making it possible for him to go on drinking." She was "preventing the crises that offer the dependent's—and the family's—one hope for change."

The oldest child is typically the *hero*, and Wegscheider makes it clear that of all the children's roles the *hero* role is most often determined by birth order. Just as Mrs. Wegscheider-Cruse fit that role in her family of origin, I did in my family. She says:

> He grows up feeling special. Parent and grandparents, aunts and uncles all dote on him. He receives more parental time and extended family attention than any of his siblings is ever likely to enjoy. This acceptance, nurturing, and support during his early developmental years provide the base of self-worth that makes possible his high performance later.

Heroes strive to be good and to achieve, whether it is sports or schoolwork or other visible effort and do so to show the world this alcoholic family is okay. However, I can't honestly say that is what motivated me to excel in school. She says that "in the alcoholic drama, the *hero* usually makes his exit early, not openly deserting the family but leaving in glory for some more distant enterprise." And I can see where I too did that. I took summer jobs out of town starting age 16 and lived away at college beginning age 18.

Dad did not achieve sobriety until I was age 23. Regarding the *hero*, Wegscheider maintains that the "goal of his achievements never is to satisfy his own needs but rather to make up for the self-worth deficit that his parents as individuals and the family as a whole are suffering." I am not convinced that that is true of me. She maintains that the *hero* feels guilty that he is not doing what he perceives he should—healing the family pain. I neither saw that in me nor did I see my parents unconsciously projecting their own guilt on me. My frustration at the realization that I could not "fix" my Dad's alcoholism was one of three key factors in my decision to accept Christ as a professing believer.

A profundity is Wegscheider's assertion that a "*hero* is not a *hero* by choice. He plays it because he must, coerced first by subtle family expectations, and later by the compulsion that results when he internalizes those expectations and makes them his own." So, I became the classic type A workaholic which she claims is a common feature of the *hero*. And remember that Wegscheider is speaking as one of these herself.

"Whatever the *hero's* pain, it rarely shows. In fact he appears to function unusually well." She points out that unless he receives help for his well-hidden pathology, he will live a life of "ignoring his own inner needs and often a stressful, success-driven lifestyle as well. Frequently one of those consequences is professional burnout." She points out that many *heroes* enter the caretaking professions. Right on! I became a physician, choosing that pathway sometime around age 17, or six years before his sobriety. By age 56 I was approaching burnout as a primary care physician who continued to be my own worst critic and be overly, sometimes unrealistically, perfectionistic.

My younger brothers fit less neatly into Wegscheider's labels, and I must credit our mother with her super-human effort to be warm and caring and individually attentive to each of us despite what she was going through with Dad's drinking. Mark, the second child at 2 years younger than I, might partly merit the *scapegoat* label. But I don't view him as having withdrawn from our family or become a delinquent. I do think he did a much better job of cultivating peer relationships than I did. Youngest brother, Mike, 10 years my junior, might merit the *mascot* label in that he was fun-loving and immature (at least until his disabling crash at age 27 caused by a drunk driver). But I don't see much else in either the *mascot* or the *lost child* roles that fit Mike. Maybe that has everything to do with my being 10 years older and pretty much out of the home by the time Mike was eight years old, hence never really getting to know him well.

Wegscheider's opening for her chapter on the *lost child* deserves focus here:

By the time the third child makes his appearance, the plot of the alcoholic drama has thickened, and the four characters already on stage are intensely involved in it. Like the *scapegoat* before him, this child feels like an outsider. Unlike the *scapegoat*, however, he does not try to force his way into the action or resort to some attention-getting tactic on another part of the stage. Instead he simply retires to the wings. Almost from infancy he senses the tensions of the drama being enacted around him, but he cannot comprehend the plot. He has arrived in the middle of the play, and no one volunteers to explain what has happened so far---family members are all too preoccupied to notice his confusion. So the little newcomer finds his own way of adapting to the situation—he gets lost.

Perhaps Mike's two extreme drunkenness episodes in the first quarter of college were manifestations of making errors in judgment because he'd had "little experience in either expressing his own feelings or handling such expressions from others." Perhaps this underlies why Mike married several times.

It may be significant that I began to preferentially use my first name (Ward, same as both my paternal grandfather and my father) in my first year of medical school after my Dad achieved lasting sobriety. Although I don't recall consciously going through this process, it is reasonable to conclude that my esteem for that name climbed immensely for the first time in my lifetime memory of family alcoholism.

I have dealt with this in some depth because I believe it's important for readers to reflect on their family roles, especially where alcoholism is present in one or more members. Being proactive in seeking restorative care for all family members, not just the *dependent* (or alcoholic) member, may head off lifetimes of residual pathology consequential to the diseased one's impact on family dynamics.

Quality speakers like Wegscheider were the norm for Awareness Hour presentations. Mr. Sharbutt told of being surprised and amazed by the impact of the Awareness Hour he and colleagues started. As a primary care physician, I had the viewpoint advantage (from an understanding point of view) of seeing alcoholism in my upbringing, but other doctors became educated by patients who had attended presentations. "We had no idea that the public would start to talk to their doctors," Sharbutt was quoted as saying. (Ref: Hazelden Betty Ford Foundation website)

Meri Bell Sharbutt, recovery mentor to Betty Ford, stated "we are trying to remove the stigma from the word 'alcoholic'...we reach people who would be frightened or embarrassed to go to an AA meeting" as key goals of their Awareness Hour programs. Mrs. Ford added: "It doesn't matter whether you start interacting with a group at a treatment center or in AA or during an Alcohol Awareness Hour; it doesn't matter whether you come through the front door or the side door or the back door; it doesn't matter whether you meet in a church basement or in a community center...there is help out there for anyone who wants it." (Ref: Betty Ford, *A Glad Awakening*, 1987)

Dad was not shy when it came to be writing those in authority on issues about which he was passionate. In April 1982, he wrote a letter to Senator Gordon Humphrey who was chairman of the Senate subcommittee on alcohol and drug abuse. Dad had been abstinent from alcohol for 16 years when his youngest son was released from a seven-month hospitalization at famed Harborview Burn Center as the then-worst-ever upper body burn victim to leave their facility alive, an on-duty Washington State trooper in a crash caused by a drunk driver. Furthermore, Dad was working now in his airline retirement as a certified alcoholism counselor. The following is an excerpt from his letter:

> As a society, we have grown to accept the deaths of Americans due to the effects of alcohol consumption as part of the cost of doing business the American way. We must reverse this cavalier attitude toward the use of alcohol. I'm sure you and your committee are aware of the effects of alcohol on the human organism. I outline a suggested avenue of approach to the solution of the alcohol/drug abuse problem.
>
> 1. Increase taxes on alcohol-containing beverages in proportion to the alcohol content, i.e. $1.00 per quart of 100 proof as a basis, 5 cents per 12 oz. beer etc.
>
> 2. Use the proceeds from #1 to establish a federally sponsored child education program to start at age 5 and continue through grade 12. This education program should be oriented toward the effects of alcohol and other drugs on the human organism, stressing the deleterious effects of these chemicals on the human's conception of reality. The education program should be factual...no preaching on the moral issues of alcohol/drug use.
>
> 3. Increase the legal drinking age to 21.
>
> 4. Change 'presumption of intoxication' from the generally accepted 0.10 BAC (author added: 0.08 BAC had not yet been legislated) to 'any detectable blood level of any mind-altering chemical.'
>
> 5. Conviction on DWI or DUI etc charges should result in:
>> (a) an automatic requirement for attendance at classes

on the effects of alcohol/drugs on the human organism

(b) evaluation of the individual by a competent practitioner to determine the extent of any alcohol or drug abuse problem with appropriate recommendation for treatment modality, etc.

(c) deprive a convicted person of his driving privileges and his right to own any type of power-driven vehicle until proof is presented that whatever problem may have been extant has been controlled.

(d) an alcohol/drug affected driver who causes death or injury should be treated the same as an individual who commits an assault with a deadly weapon.

(e) repeat offenders who have been schooled as stated in (a) or treated as in (b) and who cause death in a subsequent alcohol/drug-related accident should be subject to a charge of murder in the first degree.

(f) mandatory sentence of 5 days in jail upon conviction of DWI or DUI first offense.

(g) no plea bargaining down to a lesser charge for any offense involving alcohol or drug use.

(h) there should be no difference in the treatment of alcohol/drug-related offenses because of age. The young must be treated the same as adults. RESPONSIBILITY for one's actions must be learned the hard way if necessary. If proper schooling is provided as in (a), ignorance is no excuse.

6. Monitor all judges to insure adherence to the foregoing guidelines.

7. As costs to the Federal Government increase with the implementation of the foregoing six items, subsequent increases in federal taxes on alcohol-containing beverages would be in order. Higher cost has proven effective in reducing consumption.

8. In spite of the DISCUS (Distilled Spirits Council of the United States, an alcohol industry lobbying group...*author added*) position, all beverages containing alcohol should be labeled with a warning, i.e. 'Excessive use of this product will cause addiction to it, and dependence on it. Light to moderate use will cause impairment of judgment and rational thought. Do not attempt to drive any vehicle within 24 hours after use.'

9. Prohibit TV advertising of alcohol-containing beverages in the same manner as the prohibition of TV cigarette advertising.

These are drastic measures and any holder of political office who espouses these measures will probably be committing political suicide. An all-out effort, however, is in order. The 40 to 50-billion-dollar annual tab resulting from alcohol abuse is obscene and, in my opinion, tolerance of it is not appropriate in a civilized society. Those of us working in the Alcohol/Drug Abuse Treatment industry are truly aware of and desperately concerned with the tragic results of the lack of Federal Government guidance to the states in the solution of this problem.

One could argue that Dad's positions were extreme. To my knowledge none of the above (except the legal drinking age) have been adopted. Dad was the messenger, and the message is as clear as brother Mike's scarred disfigured body testified to the drunk driver's crime. Ingestion of alcoholic beverages is potentially damaging to the health of the user and safety of those around him. Users must be held accountable for their crimes against other innocents. Those arguing against this position are uninformed and/or motivated by selfish interests.

Ongoing aftercare is vital to the airman desiring lasting sobriety. Aftercare reporting is a key accountability force in this regard. The following is taken from American Airlines Group publication (page 34), "The HIMS Handbook," a 48-page publication revised August 2014. This segment addresses aftercare and aftercare reporting for pilots:

The people charged with ensuring safe air travel in the U.S., the FAA, require that all pilots be mentally and physically capable of piloting. Their rules are strict. Pilots who fly major carriers must have a First or Second-Class Airman Medical Certificate and have once or twice-yearly physical exam (depending on the age of the pilot) by an FAA approved physician known as an Aviation Medical Examiner (AME). No pilot who has been identified as having chemical dependence can get, or keep, an Airman Medical Certificate without completing the most effective inpatient treatment available followed by **group continuing care** for a minimum of 24 months (36 months is usual).

The FAA mandates weekly continuing care because...research shows that people who are actively involved in continuous TREATMENT of some type seem to achieve the desired goal of abstinence at a much higher rate than controls. Therefore, the FAA requires pilots to be in groups that are truly didactic treatment as opposed to groups that are just another collection of people in recovery talking about their trials and tribulations.

The only way the FAA can know about the type of continuing treatment the pilot is receiving is through written reports from the aftercare provider; so, much emphasis is placed on those reports. The FAA would like to make sure pilots are actually *involved* in the ongoing treatment, and that the aftercare counselor truly *knows* the pilot and is aware of the pilot's level of recovery progress. They would like the aftercare provider to describe the type of aftercare being provided so that the FAA can be assured it is actually treatment and not just an AA meeting without the Serenity Prayer. **As the aftercare counselor, the FAA's physicians need to be assured that you know the pilot well enough to make an informed decision about how the pilot is progressing.** Boilerplate 'checkbox' aftercare reports are unacceptable to them. The FAA psychiatrists look for the things any trained clinician would, e.g. motivation for sobriety, if the motivation is internal or external, the success the pilot has had in establishing a social system that reinforces sobriety, any signs of relapse, etc.

How you handle any known slips and relapses is a crucial piece of information and should be well described. Dr. Michael Berry of the FAA says "There is no hard and fast rule (about how to deal with relapses). The bottom line is always the quality of the recovery over a well-documented period of time."

The "Position Paper on Aftercare", authored in October 1990 by Barton Pakull, M.D., Chief Psychiatrist with the FAA, describes what the FAA wants:

"*It would be helpful if letters from the aftercare therapists at least initially describe the aftercare process.* Often the report contains no description of aftercare and the reader is wondering what is really occurring. The aftercare therapist must understand clearly that any adverse change, or even a question of an adverse change, should be reported immediately to the medical sponsor. It is also important that aftercare reports document critical issues related to sobriety for that individual. Mere statements of attendance are inadequate and may indicate a lack of familiarity with the pilot on the part of the aftercare therapist."

Put simply, the FAA psychiatrists would like to know what *you* have observed, not just how many times the pilot has attended aftercare or AA meetings.

There are two areas of confusion that need to be clarified when discussing aftercare. The first is that aftercare refers to two different but related processes. It is sometimes used to refer to the whole process of treatment (including AA) and management following the initial intensive (usually inpatient) portion of treatment. Sometimes, and especially by the Office of Aviation Medicine, it is used to refer to the specific structured outpatient treatment that occurs after the initial intensive phase. Another source of confusion is the recent use of the term 'continuing care.' It means the same thing as 'aftercare' and varies in its meaning as does aftercare. Originally, aftercare came out of the concept that following the initial inpatient treatment phase, there was a need to have further treatment on a less intense, but regular basis, that specifically addressed various issues that were beginning to be dealt with during the intensive phase. This was especially important because of the need to deal with the tendency to relapse. It gradually came to be realized that this aftercare was not just an afterthought in the treatment of alcoholism, but an integral part of the whole concept of rehabilitation. As a part of the effort to redefine the concept of treatment for alcoholism as one that is a continuous process, and to reemphasize the importance of the process of aftercare, the designation of 'continuing care' has begun to be used. It does have the advantage of emphasizing the fact that treatment needs do not end after an intensive involvement for a relatively short period of time. When the FAA process for allowing recovering alcoholic airline pilots to be returned to duty relatively soon after treatment was initiated, we had hoped to develop the program to the point where there would be a 90 % success rate. The initial success rate was good by contemporary standards, but not as good as we would have hoped. In the late seventies, the ALPA in conjunction with the FAA had a review and conference concerning the success rate, in which we specifically examined the cases where relapses had occurred. Out of this came the gradual realization that those pilots who had been in some sort of aftercare treatment did better than those who had no professional follow-up. The FAA then began to encourage an aftercare treatment phase by requiring quarterly reports from an aftercare therapist. This resulted in a decrease in percentage of relapses. Another important reason for including aftercare reports as a requirement of the exemption (special issuance) was the fact that we felt that, with a regular professional contact, we had a better chance of detecting relapses earlier than with just monitoring that depended on monthly lay observation or annual or semi-annual psychiatric evaluations.

When we examined the different varieties of aftercare experience, we quickly found that a group experience was by far the most successful. Individual aftercare therapy sessions did not appear to be very effective, especially when the frequency of the sessions dropped from weekly to monthly to every 3 months, the minimum amount of meetings necessary to fulfill the FAA special issuance requirement. Moreover, it was found that if the aftercare 'therapist' was not an alcoholism professional, and especially if the therapist had a psychoanalytic perspective, the prognosis might even be worse than not having an aftercare therapy involvement at all. We finally determined what the ideal picture of aftercare therapy should be, although we have continued to maintain flexibility about specific requirements. The ideal aftercare therapy should be an hour and a half session one evening a week. It should be a group consisting of perhaps 8-10 recovering alcoholics (or at least substance abusers) with an alcoholism professional. It should be conducted like an AA discussion group; that is, both supportive and confrontational with an emphasis on issues of adjustment related to alcoholism. These have sometimes been called 'growth groups.'

In the course of talking to airline pilots who have participated in such an aftercare experience, we have learned that not only is such an arrangement most effective for early identification of relapses, but it serves to prevent the occurrence of the relapse. It is extremely difficult for an alcoholic who is getting ready to have a relapse to attend such group sessions regularly without telegraphing the impending slip to his fellow therapy group members. Because they are dealing with the same issues and are going through the same growth process, they are more sensitive than others in picking up these early signs; it now appears that it is possible through aftercare group work to <u>even prevent the occurrence of relapses</u>. That is, the recovering pilots begin to relapse in their thinking, but it is caught and worked through <u>before they have their first drink</u>. Thus we have developed a model of group aftercare that appears to be optimal for promoting the highest success rate. We have envisioned this model as continuing for at least the first <u>2 years after return to duty</u> at which time consideration is given for reducing or eliminating all of the various monitoring requirements. However we have maintained a certain flexibility, acknowledging that in some cases it may be the Medical Sponsor's considered opinion that this much intensive aftercare participation on the part of a particular pilot is no longer necessary after a certain period of time. Therefore, although we are reluctant to accede to these recommendations and would prefer to continue on with the more intense weekly involvement, the Office of Aviation Medicine has been responsive to initiatives from Medical Sponsors to reduce the level of aftercare involvement.

There has been some resistance to this model, which has taken many forms. At first there were few aftercare groups and it was hard to find what we desired. Another problem is based upon the fact that various hospitals have developed aftercare programs because of their sincere recognition that such aftercare enhances sobriety or because it is frankly a marketing advantage to have such a program. Unfortunately, these hospital-based aftercare programs have two major disadvantages. First, the hospital tends often not to be close to where the individual resides and therefore it is difficult (and sometimes even impossible) to attend regular meetings. The second disadvantage is the fact that these hospital-based programs often provide only limited aftercare programs that run from 10 or 12 to 30 sessions and then end. We have sometimes insisted that programs keep a particular pilot in a perpetual program, recycling them through different groups. However these tend not to be as rewarding as an ongoing open-ended therapy group could be. Unfortunately, some of these so-called treatment center aftercare programs consist of nothing more than a mass AA meeting with no personal contact. We hardly consider this as coming close to meeting the objectives that we have thus far outlined. Therefore we do recommend all medical sponsors to consider initiating an aftercare group therapy program in the place where the individual pilot resides, and skipping or quickly transferring them away from the initial hospital based aftercare treatment program if it is not conveniently located. With respect to the requirement for attending weekly aftercare meetings, the objection has been made that most pilots, when they get back on an active flying schedule, are unable to make as much as 50 percent of these meetings. Therefore, it is suggested that aftercare not be required to be weekly. It is our opinion that the group sessions should remain as regularly scheduled weekly meetings so that if a pilot were able to attend only 50 percent of them, the maximum advantage would still accrue. On the other hand, if aftercare attendance was required only monthly, there would be a certain percentage that would not be able to attend that one meeting and the whole emphasis on a continuing confrontational/supportive relationship would be lost.

Some airlines have group meetings within their domiciles, usually in the nature of combining the monthly contacts by supervisors and peers with employee assistance program (EAP) and medical input. These are recognized to be very successful in reinforcing sobriety as well as being a monitoring technique that is extremely effective. However we do not feel that these represent specific aftercare experiences of a therapeutic nature, and feel that even with these kinds of programs within certain airlines, an aftercare program as we have described it should be maintained.

Some pilots choose to (or are advised to) undergo marital therapy or individual therapy for various issues which may contribute to or have an impact on their alcoholism problem. We normally do not request that these kinds of voluntary (or semi-voluntary) individual treatment experiences be a part of monitoring. We feel that this experience is enhanced if separated from monitoring, and we never make them a requirement for special issuance. Therefore, when individuals choose to be in an individual or couples therapy experience, we would prefer they nevertheless engage in a group aftercare experience. In that way they can end or modify their personal therapy as they need to, without external pressures from the FAA that would not be therapeutic.

Aftercare is not a substitute for AA. Even though AA attendance is not required and not a part of monitoring, we recognize its importance to maintaining the quality of sobriety necessary for aviation safety. In terms of arranging aftercare it would be most helpful if the sponsor were to plan ahead while the pilot was still in the inpatient intensive phase so that there could be a smooth transition into a permanent aftercare relationship. The sponsor should receive monthly aftercare reports until such time as the case is ready for presentation to the FAA. In this way, progress in areas crucial to recovery can be closely followed. It would be helpful if letters from the aftercare therapist at least initially describe the aftercare process. Often the report contains no description of aftercare and the reader is left wondering what is really occurring. After the special issuance is granted, there must be written reports at least quarterly from the aftercare therapist to the medical sponsor. Of course the aftercare therapist must understand clearly that any adverse change, or even a question of an adverse change, should be reported immediately to the medical sponsor. It is also important that aftercare reports do document critical issues related to sobriety for that individual. Mere statements of attendance are inadequate, and may indicate a lack of familiarity with the pilot on the part of the aftercare therapist.

It appears there is a growing trend toward an increase in relapses after the first two years, when monitoring is relaxed. This may mean that we should be very cautious about ending such a successful mode of relapse prevention as group aftercare, merely because an individual has achieved two years of abstinence after returning to duty. In summary, the ideal aftercare treatment program consists of a group that meets in a locality that is convenient to the pilot, on a weekly basis, and preferably for at least all of the first two years.

CHAPTER EIGHT
BE ONE, SEE ONE, TEACH ONE

Pan Am retirement freed up more time to devote to the cause that now consumed Dad: helping others to the recovery phase he now so enjoyed. While no longer an active flying airman and an ALPA leader, he was still in demand from around the globe to help others trapped in the bondage of addiction. Although he had an engineering degree acquired prior to his airline career, he decided to go to school at Seattle University to become a certified alcoholism counselor. Several papers he wrote during that time are in my possession and provide further insight into his own disease experience and recovery. While there is some redundancy of details, I will not alter what he submitted in order that you see his world as he perceived it at the time that he wrote these documents.

This first paper titled "ALCOHOL AND THE AIRLINE AIRMAN" was written spring quarter 1978 for a college course, "Survey on Alcoholism." Note his data on reasons for Pan Am pilots being removed from seniority listing which is placed in his Epilogue at the paper's conclusion. Forty-three pilots of the 347 removed from that list prior to Dad's March 1978 mandatory age 60 retirement were terminated for alcohol-related reasons. He emphasizes that represents a 12.4% incidence, but it does not include recovered airmen (like himself) or ones who successfully continued to hide their disease. Such data do suggest that alcoholism is in fact more common amongst flight crew than the usually cited 10% incidence for the general population.

Dad's paper is reproduced in its entirety and comprises the next six pages, ending with his bibliography of references used for writing it.

ALCOHOL AND THE AIRLINE AIRMAN

Who cannot recall the classic portrayal of the World Ward I ace returning to his home base   from a daring mission, landing his shot-tattered SPAD and proceeding forthwith to the squadron club where toasts were hoisted to fellow airmen who did not return, or courage renewed to fly and fight again at dawn? Thus, a cavalier attitude associated booze with flying in the minds of many.

The use of alcohol by the flight crew has not been cited as a factor in any U.S. air carrier accident. The same cannot be said of foreign carriers, general aviation or the U.S. military (1). Documented cases exist however in which airline airmen have been forcibly removed from their aircraft prior to flight when intoxication was detected by other members of the operating crew (i.e. crew members responsible for actual manipulation of aircraft flight systems).

Original federal regulations pertaining to the use of alcohol prohibited an individual from operating an aircraft while intoxicated. Subsequent revisions of the regulations produced the current eight-hour rule (2) which prohibits a crew member from acting as such within 8 hours after the consumption of any alcoholic beverage. This regulation presumes that alcoholism does not exist in the airman group since FAR Part 67 defines alcoholism: "a diagnosable disease in those whose alcohol intake is great enough to damage physical health, or personal or social functioning (which includes occupational functioning), or when it has become a prerequisite to normal functioning (3)."

Gamma alcoholism (4) is characterized by loss of control of the amount ingested, once commenced, and is believed to be the predominating species of alcoholism in the U.S. How can an alcoholic airman be expected to stop drinking eight hours prior to flight if he has 'lost control'? Should the alcoholic airman exercise sufficient control to stop alcohol intake in compliance with the regulation, he is then subject to 'withdrawal syndrome' (4,5) which may be characterized by disturbances in the central nervous system such as grand mal, epileptiform convulsions, hallucinations, disorientation, etc., a highly undesirable event to occur anywhere, least of all in the cockpit of an airplane. This has occurred, but the fail-safe concept of multiple-member flight crew prevented serious consequence except to the individual so affected.

If the disease has progressed sufficiently in the individual, it is quite likely that he can perform his function with greater skill if he maintains the proper blood alcohol level (5) ...i.e. within his tolerance limit. However, the tolerance limit has been demonstrated to lie within a very narrow band and varies with hunger, blood sugar fluctuations, fatigue, stress or preoccupation with emotionally charged activities (5). Thus, self-dosage to maintain the proper blood level is doomed to failure due to the many variables involved. Let us for a moment presume that an airman of 170 pounds with a 'normal' liver function consumes enough alcohol to render himself close to unconsciousness and retires to 'sleep it off' eight hours prior to flight. He could very well have a blood Alcohol content (BAC) of 0.30% to 0.35% at that time. His system is detoxified at an average rate of 0.015% (6) per hour. Using the lower BAC of 0.30%, he is still legally 'under the influence' in most states (i.e. 0.10% BAC) after 13 hours. However, he has complied with the so-called 'eight-hour rule' and regards himself as not in violation. Federal Aviation Regulation 91.11 (2) prohibits acting as a crew member 'while under the influence of alcohol.' The individual in the example is 'under the influence' but doesn't know it since he believes the 'eight-hour rule' is more restrictive. In the cited example, the individual's body would not be free of alcohol until 20 hours after he stopped drinking. Based on the foregoing, the author regards the so-called 'eight-hour rule' as either self-defeating or ineffective if enhancement of air safety is the prime consideration.

TO RESTATE THE DILEMMA:

The sufferer from Alpha alcoholism (4) thinks he has complied with regulations by stopping his alcohol intake eight hours prior to flight duty when in fact he may, depending upon the rate of ingestion and total amount ingested, have an appreciable BAC after eight hours. The sufferer from Gamma alcoholism (4) cannot be depended upon to comply with the regulation because of the very nature of the disease. If he does comply, his exposure to the withdrawal syndrome does not further the cause of air safety. All the foregoing serves to further point out the fallacy in the attempt to control alcohol abuse and to solve the problems of alcoholism by law, regulation, work rule or edict.

HOPE FOR THE FUTURE?

Early comprehensive education of the airman on the subject of alcohol and its effect on the human organism may be efficacious for those who still have the freedom of choice (7). Completion of such education could be made a requirement for initial employment. Services of the NIAAA National Center for Alcohol Education (NCAE) could be utilized to this end (8).

ARE AIRMEN MORE AT RISK THAN THE GENERAL POPULATION?

Those most likely to be heavy drinkers are men who have completed high school and men who did not finish college (9). Statistics show all airline airmen have completed high school and the average college level is three years (10). The highest proportion of heavy drinkers (30%) is found among men aged 30-34 and 45-49. The median age for the airline airmen group is 42.28 (9). Two alcoholism inhibiting factors (11) are missing from the airline airman's life:

1. A close knit family life with little or no traveling by family members

2. An income level which limits the major portion of expenditures to necessities

Most airline airmen are acquired from the military, thus excepting the airlines from initial training costs. Captain Joseph A. Pursch, Director...Long Beach Naval Hospital Alcohol and Drug Rehabilitation Center, has determined that 38% of the navy's officers and enlisted men are heavy drinkers and have serious problems as a result (12). There is no reason to believe other military services would experience a lower incidence. Reliable survey figures for the U.S. Army and Air Force are conspicuous by the absence of their availability.

Some job-related factors conducive to the development of alcoholism may be (11):

1. Lack of visibility on the job

2. Lack of direct supervision

3. Absence of job structure

4. No evaluation of work

5. Flexible work patterns

6. Freedom to set work hours

7. Little or no social controls

8. Occupational obsolescence or job degradation

9. A stress and strain occupation

Every factor with the exception of number four (which is preceded by notification far in advance) is present in the airman's profession with special emphasis on number nine which, it is felt, is of particular significance in the development of the disease in airmen (13). Stress factors are:

1. Peak work load at varying times

2. Necessity of maintaining high awareness over long time periods

3. Constant noise and vibrations

4. Very low humidity

5. Time zone changes of eight or more hours in a single flight which disturbs body rhythms and sleep patterns

6. Mechanical and weather problems with resultant schedule disruptions

7. Irregular eating times

8. Lack of proper rest facilities at layover points

The author believes that the use of the job-related factors in references 12 and 13 by an individual to justify resorting to alcohol is a cop-out. These factors provide the excuse to drink and a dangerous pattern may be established leading to reliance on alcohol rather than reality for relief. It therefore appears evident that the airline airman is more at risk than the general male population.

HISTORIC HANDLING OF DETECTED ALCOHOLISM AND/OR ALCOHOL ABUSE INVOLVING AN AIRLINE AIRMAN:

A diagnosis of alcoholism or a history of 'excessive drinking habit' disqualifies any airman from possession of the FAA medical certificate required for his employment. Therefore an airman so diagnosed must obtain from the Federal Air Surgeon a grant of exemption to Federal Aviation Regulations (3). No exemptions were granted until 1973 when one was obtained. Consequently, the airlines and the labor organizations representing the airman ignored alcohol abuse and alcoholism, thus becoming 'enablers' (14) in the most classic sense. When overt action on the part of the sick airman brought attention to his condition, management usually fired him. The labor organization tried to defend him, usually in vain. The Federal Aviation Agency was always, to the extent possible, kept out of the act. Were the FAA to be part of the act, the airlines and labor organizations would have to admit that their airmen did use alcohol and, being human, did develop problems with alcohol. Meanwhile most of the airmen involved soon died and created no further problem. However, a few airmen miraculously recovered before their cases were irreversible, and these few formed a nucleus of hope for others. The few who did recover avoided the grant of exemption procedure since an attempt to comply would deprive them of their livelihood. A low profile was maintained, and they participated in clandestine efforts designed to guide other troubled airmen to sobriety.

Prior to 1972 no carrier had accepted the disease concept of alcoholism as applicable to airmen. Prior to 1974 no airman labor organization had accepted the disease concept. Professional standards and moral grounds were regarded as sufficient deterrents to the acquisition of alcohol-related problems.

COMES THE DAWN

Early in 1974 the Air Line Pilots Association obtained a grant from NIAAA (15) to conduct a study of alcohol abuse and alcoholism as pertains to airmen. The resultant Human Intervention and Motivation Study-ALPA, under the direction of R. L. Masters, M.D., Aero medical Advisor to the ALPA, has been gratifyingly successful in setting up effective model programs on many airlines. These programs are tailored to the specific needs of licensed airmen (enc. A & B). The Federal Air Surgeon, H. L. Reighard, issued a bulletin titled 'Alcoholism and Airline Flight Crew Members' dated Nov. 10, 1976 (enc. C) providing specific treatment guidelines and streamlining the grant of exemption procedure, providing adherence to certain stringent conditions is maintained.

Today, every air carrier in the U.S. has endorsed the disease concept of alcoholism and is participating in cooperation with the Federal Aviation Agency and airmen labor organizations in efforts to control the disease. Every air carrier, that is, with the glaring exception of one whose chief executive officer espouses the time-worn euphemism...*oh, we don't have any problem with alcoholics, we fire them* (7). A successful approach to the control of alcohol abuse and alcoholism must have the full support of management and labor organizations (7,16).

Much has been accomplished in the last eighteen months through the coordinated efforts of many. Reluctant managements have been successfully persuaded and many airmen have recovered. Follow-up has shown these men to be more effective employees as a result of their illness than they were before alcohol became a problem. The Federal Air Surgeon's bulletin (enc. D) seemed to provide the spark needed for a coordinated effort. However, the danger area delineated on pages 1, 2 and 3 of this paper remains extant. Massive educational efforts must be forthcoming properly directed in a manner acceptable to the airman who still has a choice. If this is not accomplished, we will see the day when each airman will be required to submit to a BAC test upon reporting for duty. There comes a time when the civil rights of a few must be set aside to enhance the safety of many.

The following quote from Robert C. Hickle seems appropriate in conclusion:

> I stand in my garden, ready to plant peas. I have spaded it, raked it, fertilized it, and the calendar says today is the day to plant peas. I look at the pea in my hand. Green, hard, wrinkled, dry. No life of any kind shows.
> Yet, if I want to raise a patch of peas, this is what I plant. I dig the trench, lay in the peas and cover them. My job is over. I can go fishing, watch TV or sleep, but I cannot do anything to make that pea grow. The sun will shine, the ground will get warm and the rain will fall. I have that faith. I can pull the weeds and chase off the rabbits, and I can help out the rain with the garden hose, but nothing in the world I can do will make those peas grow, blossom and bear.
> So it is with the alcoholic. We prepare the ground, plant the seed and pull the weeds, but there is nothing we can do to make it grow. Just as with the peas, the life lies within the alcoholic. We know we won't help any alcoholic if we don't plant the seed, but only God can make it grow. When we start giving instructions to God on how to make the seed grow, we are out of our field. That's His! And when a seed doesn't sprout, that's His too! Maybe another time, another growing season, it will sprout. And maybe never. It's not for us to say which shall grow and which not, any more than we can make any of them grow.

Ours is to plant the seed. His is to make it grow (17).

EPILOGUE

The author recently retired from a major air carrier following more than 36 years as a command pilot. At the time of his initial employment, he was the last employed of 375 airmen with that carrier (i.e. seniority number 375). At the time of his retirement, his relative position on the seniority list was number 28 which means that 347 airmen were removed from the seniority prior to the author's retirement. An airman is removed from the seniority list when he leaves employment as an airman with the company. This event occurs for the following reasons:

1) Airman reaches mandatory retirement age 60

2) Airman fails to successfully accomplish any one of three comprehensive physical examinations required each year

3) Airman fails to accomplish proficiency checks required thrice annually (i.e. incompetence)

4) Discharge for rules infractions

5) Resignation

6) Death

Of the 347 airmen removed from the seniority list prior to author's retirement at age 60, 43 airmen careers were terminated prior to normal retirement due to various sequel of alcohol abuse and alcoholism. Perhaps more airmen were similarly affected. However the author's personal knowledge extends only to the number mentioned. This number demonstrates an incidence of 12.4% and does not include recovered airmen nor those in whom the disease was successfully hidden through their careers.

The author is a recovered alcoholic.

REFERENCES

1. A.F. Zeller, Aviation Space Environmental Medicine 46 (10), 1271-1274, 1975
2. Federal Aviation Regulations Part 91.11
3. Federal Aviation Regulations Part 67
4. E. M. Jellinek, The Disease Concept of Alcoholism, chapter 3
5. James R. Milam, The Emergent Comprehensive Concept on Alcoholism, p.14-15 & 18
6. Blood Alcohol Concentration, Washington State Liquor Control Board
7. Smithers Foundation, Understanding Alcoholism, Chapter 6 & 7
8. Alcohol World, winter 77-78 vol. 2, no. 2, p.22
9. Alcohol & Health, HEW, chapter 2
10. Airline Pilots Association...membership statistics, Wash DC
11. Capt. J.A.Pursch,USN,M.D.,Naval Aviation News, March 1974
12. Trice & Roman, Spirits & Demons at Work, 1972, IV:101-120
13. ALPA, Human Intervention and Motivation Study, Denver CO. Company program guidance
14. V. E. Johnson, I'll Quit Tomorrow, 5:47
15. NIAAA Information & Feature Service IFS #45, March3 1978
16. R. A. Von Wiegand, N.C.A. Preventive Medicine 1974, 3:80-85
17. R. C. Hickle, Responsible Drinking and Other Myths, p.29"

The one airline outlier referred to above was Northwest Airlines whose CEO, Donald Nyrop, was famously quoted as saying "Oh, we don't have any problem with alcoholics, we just fire them." The 1990 widely publicized arrest of the three-man NWA crew for flying impaired made converts out of NWA management then. How ironic that a lengthy article in the February 6, 1979, issue of the Minneapolis Star newspaper written by John Oslund should address the subject of airlines' approach to alcoholic pilots! That author included much information critical of NWA's approach then to alcohol dependent pilots. He quotes Dr. Richard Masters then as stating: "We have considerable amount of concern about the cases at Northwest, we are very worried about the need for pilots who may have problems with alcoholism and we feel the company's position is certainly inhumane and, I would say, irresponsible." He went on to say: "If a Northwest pilot declares to the FAA, he will be unable to return to flying because Northwest will refuse to allow him to. I can't say enough for my contempt for the policy at Northwest. The guys need help, and they need to get help, and they probably are. But they are not coming through this office because we would jeopardize our whole program if we dealt under the counter for Northwest pilots." This article went on to state: "Northwest is the only major US airline that doesn't have a program, according to Dr. H. L. Reighard FAA Air Surgeon, the agency's top medical authority." Note that Northwest was headquartered in Minneapolis where this newspaper was also located. "Reighard came to Minneapolis to explain the program to Northwest's then-chairman, Donald Nyrop. But Nyrop was not persuaded." Reighard was quoted as follows: "The company notified us that it will not participate in a monitoring program."

A term paper for the 1978 Fall quarter class, Personal and Social Rehabilitation of the Alcoholic, was composed and titled "REFLECTIONS ON COMPLEXITY." Engineers are typically not given to deep thinking on matters of a philosophical nature and Dad was such a man. But here he cites several authors from the realms of philosophy and psychology before giving us personal insight into himself and his alcoholism. Incidentally, Bill W. referred to at outset was a co-founder of Alcoholics Anonymous. I have chosen to reproduce Dad's original 1978 writing in its entirety unaltered, and it comprises three and a half pages that now follow:

REFLECTIONS ON COMPLEXITY

I quote in part from Dr. C.G.Jung's letter to Bill W. dated January 30, 1961:

His craving for alcohol was the equivalent, on a low level, of the spiritual thirst of our being for wholeness, expressed in medieval language: the union with God. How could one formulate such an insight in a language that is not misunderstood in our days? The only right and legitimate way to such an experience is that it happens to you in reality, and it can only happen to you when you walk on a path which leads you to higher understanding. You might be led to that goal by an act of grace or through a personal and honest contact with friends, or through a higher education of the mind beyond the confines of mere rationalism. I see from your letter that Roland H. has chosen the second way which was, under the circumstances, obviously the best one. I am strongly convinced that the evil principle prevailing in this world leads the unrecognized spiritual need into perdition if it is not counteracted either by real religious insight or by the protective wall of human community. An ordinary man, not protected by an action from above and isolated in society, cannot resist the power of evil, which is called very aptly the Devil. But the use of such words arouses so many mistakes that one can only keep aloof from them as much as possible. These are the reasons why I could not give a full and sufficient explanation to Roland H., but I am risking it with you because I conclude from your very decent and honest letter that you have acquired a point of view above the misleading platitudes one usually hears about alcoholism. You see, 'alcohol' in Latin is 'spiritus,' and you use the same word for the highest religious experience as well as for the most depraving poison. The helpful formula therefore is: 'spiritus contra spiritum.'

R. G. Bell observes in Escape from Addiction: "...as we enter the final third of the 20th century there is conclusive evidence that our affluent society is failing to meet the basic physical, psychological, social and spiritual needs of its members.....I believe that the healthiest humans are those who can harness their intelligence most effectively in a balanced concern for themselves and the species." To acquire happiness, Bell says balanced attention is required in three levels of territorial behavior: "activities that involve the intimate relationships of family or friends which provide most of the joy and security in human experience; activities concerned with personal survival, food, possessions and status which fulfill the territorial need for a minimum of personal living space and are an important factor in personal identity; activities which have been concerned with the common good of the group.....we need a cause above self, a reason for effort over and above the demands of family, friends and possessions."

Glasser says that antisocial or aberrant behavior by an individual is the result of the individual being unable to fulfill his essential human needs plus the denial of reality. He feels that the need to love and be loved and the need to feel we are worthwhile to ourselves and others are basic psychological needs. A feeling of one's responsibility toward humanity is essential.

Vernon Johnson says of recovery: "by behaving properly, a person can meet his own needs and other persons' as well. The goal is a triple one: (1) to know oneself at a feeling level, (2) to know the feelings of others, (3) to combine these insights for the benefit of both. Personal insight leads to the ability to be accurately empathetic, which in turn leads to the ability to choose appropriate actions; which leads finally to deepening interpersonal relationships."

Eric Hoffer observes: "in a man's life, the lack of an essential component usually leads to the adoption of a substitute. The substitute is usually embraced with vehemence and extremism...Man's only legitimate end in life is to finish God's work...to bring to full growth the capacities and talents implanted in us....All that schoolmasters can teach in a classroom is as nothing when compared with what we cannot help teaching each other in honest personal interaction. There is no dividing line between learning and living." Hoffer continues: "A feeling of utter worthlessness levels a man's attitude toward his fellow beings. He views the whole of humanity as being of one kind. He will despise and fear equally those who love him and those who hate him, those who are noble and those who are mean, those who are compassionate and those who are cruel. It is as though the feeling of worthlessness cuts one off from the rest of mankind, and humanity is seen as a foreign species. What are we when we are alone? Some, when alone, cease to exist. The end comes when we no longer talk with ourselves. It is the end of genuine thinking and the beginning of the final loneliness. The remarkable thing is that the cessation of the inner dialogue marks also the end of our concern with the world around us. It is as if we note the world and think about it only when we have to report to ourselves. The hopeful can draw strength from the most ridiculous sources of power...a slogan, a word, a button. No faith is potent unless it is also faith in the future. The burning conviction that we have a holy duty toward others is often a way of attaching our drowning selves to a passing raft. What looks like giving a hand is often a holding on for dear life. Take away our holy duties and our lives are left puny and meaningless. There is no doubt that in exchanging a self-centered for a selfless life we gain enormously in self-esteem."

Simone Weil states: "those who serve a cause are not those who love that cause. They are those who love the life which must be led in order to serve it...for the idea of a cause does not supply the necessary energy required for serving it."

Emerson said: "in every man there is something wherein I may learn of him; and in that I am his pupil. When genius speaks to us, we feel a ghostly reminiscence of having ourselves, in the distant past, had vaguely this self-same thought which genius now speaks, but which we had not art or courage to clothe with form and utterance."

The lecture on Moreno's "Social Atom," presented October 24, 1978, is in combination with the foregoing quotes "How It Works." I confess that during Lorie Dwinell's lecture, Emerson's stated quote flashed as lightning in my recollection. Speaking from my personal experience with alcohol and from close association with others similarly affected, the alcoholic at the end of his drinking career may be likened to an island awash in a raging sea. An island, so positioned, cannot long exist before it is washed away and naught remains. Perhaps a better analogy would be "advancing alone into chaos in the dark." In any case the alcoholic has systematically cut himself off from every meaningful human relationship due to the distortion of his thinking and judgmental processes by alcohol. The only meaningful relationship left is with alcohol which now does things to him, not for him. I would prefer to use the term "social molecule" for an individual in that it is easier for me to visualize a molecule divesting itself of atoms, one at a time, thus becoming an unrecognizable replica of the former self.

For those of us who had a reasonably normal and successful life until alcohol became a severe problem, I feel that the transition to sobriety is easier than for one who develops the problem early in life since in a rare moment of spiritual awareness we may remember that life was at one time good and be prompted to surrender unconsciously to reality. The younger person may have nothing in his past to motivate him to 'a return to normalcy,' and the surrender in these cases may be prompted more by physical than psychic pain. I feel that the younger person may be harder to convince of his need for other humans and without the recognition of one's need for deep spiritual attachment with other humans there may be little chance of recovery. When I came to Alcoholics Anonymous, my self-esteem was at level zero. When I looked into the mirror on my last day of drinking, there was nothing recognizable looking back. I had destroyed, through the use of alcohol, every relationship that was meaningful to me. Stripped of the relationships that make each human unique, the entity had been reduced to an amorphous glob. At that point, the process of surrender occurred as described by H. M. Tiebout: "It is to be viewed as a moment when the unconscious forces of defiance and grandiosity actually cease effectively to function. When that happens, the individual is wide open to reality; he can listen and learn without conflict and fighting back. He is receptive to life, not antagonistic. He senses a feeling of relatedness and at-oneness which becomes the source of an inner peace, the possession of which frees the individual from the compulsion to drink. In other words, an act of surrender is an occasion wherein the individual no longer fights life but accepts it.... It is now possible to define the emotional state of surrender as a state in which there is a persisting capacity to accept reality. In this definition, the capacity to accept reality must not be conceived of in a passive sense, but in the active sense of reality being a place where one can live and function as a person acknowledging one's responsibilities and feeling free to make that reality more livable for oneself and others....With true unconscious surrender, the acceptance of reality means the individual can work in it with it. The state of surrender is really positive and creative."

The people in the fellowship of A.A. accepted me and loved me in spite of my alcoholism, but they could not accept my need for continued use of alcohol. I began to respect these people since they had what I wanted. As my respect for these people grew, my self-esteem began to return through association. I was one of the group I respected, ergo, it followed my self-respect was warranted. I learned that love is affectionate concern for the well-being of another and does not necessarily have a sexual connotation. A comfortable at-oneness with God followed and my former demands for help turned to expressions of deep gratitude to Him for His guidance wherever it may lead. By conducting my life so as to fall within the limits indicated by the fourth step inventory, personal growth made possible the extension of the inventory limits (step 10) and gradual progress was made toward the state of being 'weller than well.' Logical progression in attempting to practice the principles of A.A. in all facets of life brought me to the point of possibly being useful in helping others to recover from alcoholism.

It has been said that "nothing so educates as does a shock." I am thankful that the shock of my powerlessness over alcohol provided the impetus for learning the true meaning of a full and satisfying life, maintaining constant awareness of Hoffer's admonition "our triviality is proportionate to the seriousness with which we take ourselves." My goal is success as defined by Emerson:

> To laugh often and much;
> To win the respect of intelligent people and the affection of children;
> To earn the appreciation of honest critics and
> To endure the betrayal of false friends;
> To appreciate beauty and to find the best in others;
> To leave the world a bit better, whether by a healthy child, a garden patch or a redeemed social condition,
> To know even one life has breathed easier because you have lived.
> This is to have succeeded.

"Group Dynamics in Alcohol Treatment," a summer quarter 1980 course, generated the following from Dad's pen. His conclusions are provocative and insightful. Recall that he was a 'control freak' and we three boys emulated his example to a large extent. One might expect control freaks would have difficulties interacting with groups, especially when the groupthink was at odds with the conclusions of the control freak. His composition, which comprises a little over one page in length, follows now unaltered:

> Having been recently somewhat traumatized by the negative stroke of a federal judge's pen nullifying ten years group effort in the aviation industry's facing up to alcoholism problems pertaining to airmen, I found myself in need of a new experience. Positive reinforcement? One way or another, we all depend on feedback.
>
> In any case I was determined to lay back and not function in any leadership capacity inasmuch as through school and my working career most groups of which I was a member were task oriented and seemed to select me in some leadership role, a position not always coveted. My intention was to observe and learn without participation. However, I found I could not remain detached and still attain the course objectives as stated. In addition it became evident that such a course of action would be unfair to the teacher as well as the class members.

I'm not at all sure that the 'fish bowl' results as experienced in this class would be considered as representative of a general 'run of the mill' group. It is my opinion that this class is made up of feeling people or at least a majority of those wanting to be in touch on a feeling level. I was astounded that a group spirit and feeling of cohesiveness developed so quickly and suspect this to be due to the expertise of the teacher. All class members appear to feel a group identity.

My previous group experiences have involved dealing with special interest subgroups within the main group. I don't sense any particular special interest people in our class with the possible exception of two who seem to have some bias, but perhaps more effort at personal interaction on my part would prove my impression to be in error.

The random selection of the subgroups gave me a feeling of apprehension since I had already made up my mind (a faulty trait) about the two aforementioned individuals and didn't want to share with them on a feeling level. Still don't but since I feel comfortable with fifteen out of seventeen, I'm not too concerned. I must admit to a vague sense of loss in not endeavoring to know them better.

The subgroup of which I was a member developed an immediate sense of cohesiveness and decided unanimously not to be a task force but to share on a feeling level with one another and acknowledge no group leader. The philosophy of the group was aptly stated by one member: 'Let everyone do his or her thing. I don't want anyone to tell me what to do, nor do I want anyone to tell what to do.' Sounds like anarchy but no problems of procedure, jurisdiction of turf or bonding in pairs occurred in a manner that could disrupt the group. It was a very rewarding experience.

Diagnosis in retrospect is a somewhat difficult and futile exercise. However, this course has enabled me to look back on groups of which I was a member and make a determination as to why some were more effective than others in attaining an objective. A great truth has dawned...some groups are doomed to failure regardless of the competence of the leader and intelligence of the members and this is due to the dynamics of the personalities involved.

I feel participation in this class will better equip me to conduct future group activities. This has been an experience I'll not soon forget and deserves a better paper than time permits me to prepare.

What follows was a part of Dad's 3-ring binder of saved documents from his Seattle University course days but bears no date or course title. The concluding portion gives further insight into his personal battle with alcoholism, and he is the author of what now follows reproduced unaltered and comprising nearly two pages:

There is ample archeological and geological evidence showing the existence of alcohol (ethanol) on Earth as long ago as the late Paleozoic era, at least two hundred million years ago. Its use was confined to mammalian ancestors of man until the appearance of homo sapiens in the form of Neanderthal man during the mid Paleolithic period between 100,000 and 40,000 years back.

Ingestion of fermented honey from a fallen bee tree probably led to the discovery of alcohol's effect in altering the state of human consciousness. The effects of the drug were so startling that spiritual qualities were attributed to it. It became a part of religious rites, and it is thought that the manufacture of alcoholic drink from grains and fruit became the responsibility of the spiritual leaders. Inebriety or drunkenness was permitted only as part of certain religious festivities.

The casual use of alcohol, like the individual chronic inebriate, seems to be a product of civilization. Recorded history in the form of clay tablets dating back to the third pre-Christian millennium and found near the head of the Persian gulf contain reference to "beer and bread for one day" as part of the wage allowance for labor. Somewhat less ancient Mesopotamian accounts of the Flood indicate that Noah thoughtfully included beer and wine in the provisioning of the Ark. With regard to Noah, the Old Testament makes reference to his familiarity with alcohol by saying '...and he drank of the wine and was drunken.'

The first written regulations as to the use of alcohol were promulgated by the Mesopotamian Hammurabi around 2300 B.C. Also the first clinical description of intoxication was recorded at this time as well as a cure for hangovers. History indicates that the Egyptians were beginning to encounter alcohol-related problems at the same time. Oriental history seems to indicate the presence of a built-in defense mechanism within that ethnic group. Ingestion of alcohol causes much physical discomfort and the mental effect doesn't make the discomfort worthwhile. Jews, probably due to their youthful exposure to Egyptian culture, denounced drunkenness but held alcohol in good esteem and on occasion would prescribe it for various ills. The Greeks and Romans in their turn have issued their cautions regarding habitual and excessive use of intoxicants.

It's well to remember that the alcoholic beverages referred to thus far were made from honey, beer from grain and wine from fruit. The alcohol content in all is limited to 14% by virtue of the yeast's tolerance to alcohol. When the alcohol content reaches 14%, the yeast dies and the process of fermentation ceases. How to raise the alcohol content of a given volume of drink? The discovery of the process of distillation is attributed to an Arabian alchemist known as Geber but distillation was not widely used in beverage production until the Frenchman Villeneuve in about 1400 applied the process to wine and produced aqua vitae...water of life, which we know as brandy. The medical community of that time greeted the liquid with tremendous enthusiasm, and its prescription for almost every illness rivaled the current enthusiasm in the prescription of the minor tranquilizers. The manufacture of whiskey, gin and vodka followed quickly. In England the demand for distilled spirits exceeded available supply to such a degree that the British government in 1690 enacted a law encouraging increased production of distilled spirits, and in forty years its production increased by a factor of 25. Sensing trouble by reference to widespread public drunkenness and violence, the government attempted to control alcohol abuse by leveling prohibitive taxes on the beverage so as to make it unaffordable and also encouraged a fledgling temperance movement. The New World provided a new beverage...rum. However the first visitors to both North and South America found that the products of fermentation had preceded them. Again the native population ascribed spiritual qualities to the beverages and use was confined to religious rites. Quite likely, the liquid was in short supply as well.

Let's now skip to the times somewhat more familiar to us as denoted by this forerunner of the bumper sticker and marking the end of the "noble experiment" or the Volstead Act and providing my introduction to the elixir of life newly available in 3.2 beer. The harder stuff was available but my financial constraints exacted a type of prohibition. Now any substance whose ingestion produces an altered state of consciousness is <u>psychologically addictive</u> if the individual finds enjoyment in his or her altered state. Does alcohol alter the state of human consciousness? It was widely used by the British navy as an anesthetic for surgical procedures. The only problem in its use as an anesthetic is the fact that enough to provide deep anesthesia is very close to the amount which produces death. Being, as are most humans, a hedonist, I enjoyed alcohol's effect in that reality was presented in a much more acceptable perspective. Alcohol did something for me that it apparently does not do for the vast majority of people who drink. Had I known at the time what I subsequently was taught, perhaps I would not have become alcoholic. In any case, the warning was there unheeded. Alcoholism did develop and I now believe it was God's plan for me to be reduced to helplessness in order to be reborn to learn His plan for a life leading to the happiness I was forever seeking in the bottle. Rather a paradox. It has been said that nothing so educates as does a shock and the shock of the realization of my powerlessness regarding the use of alcohol was devastating.

Addiction is characterized by dependence on the chemical, an increase in tolerance to it and withdrawal symptoms when its use is stopped. In retrospect I see that my addiction was mainly psychological. Certain physical deterioration had manifested itself. However nothing in the text of the classic physical withdrawal syndrome occurred.

The people in AA told me that I had a disease...alcoholism. Does alcoholism meet disease criteria? I think it does since it causes illness, can be diagnosed and can be treated. They also told me that, if untreated, alcoholism is 100% fatal. Further, AA's told me I would never have to drink again <u>one day at a time</u> provided I followed the twelve steps they had followed. They also promised an enjoyment of life I never dreamed existed. They also promised that I would grow to enjoy reality and would be able to cope with any eventuality <u>one day at a time</u> provided I followed their steps. They were right.

CHAPTER NINE
CHALLENGE TO READERS PLUS HELPING RESOURCES

I leave you, the flying public, with a serious challenge. While the story I've told is encouraging in the sense that government regulators, company management and pilot unions are now unified in seeking to find, treat and rehabilitate alcohol dependent airmen, the very subject of everyone's attention sometimes is still hiding his or her disease. We know that is true because of nearly annual news reports of impaired pilots discovered on the job. Why is it that some alcoholism-diseased individuals persist in denying and hiding their disease when the three unified parties listed above are affirmingly outspoken about their desire to help and heal these airmen?

The answer is simple---yet profound. Those same airmen are still human beings submerged in the trappings of alcoholism's grip, and some around them are often though unwittingly enabling them, thus helping support their addictive lifestyle rather than allowing the inevitable crises that often serve to drive those in need to seek help.

I implore those surrounding the still-in-denial alcoholic airman, whether it be family or friends or fellow crew members or their family doctor or dentist, to seek the help of those experienced in conducting interventions. Don't be afraid to meet with their work supervisor to explain reality and enlist their help by bringing the threat of job loss as a big stick to motivate airmen to admit their need for treatment and rehabilitation. End-stage alcoholism is a poor second choice line of action (better labeled as "inaction"). The practicing alcoholic, mired deep in the pit of his addictive lifestyle, is in no position to make it on his own until the perpetual two carbon pickling is allowed to clear from his system; and until those already recovered are recruited to assist in progressively leading him or her toward the serenity of a salvaged life free of booze.

Realize too that airline pilots are clearly at increased risk for becoming alcohol dependent. While lengthy layovers at points distant from home are less common in this jet age than during the pre-jet era of flight, family life and regular sleep routines for many pilots are still disrupted by flight schedules. Overnight layovers far from home invite the crew to socialize as a group, often in a bar or cocktail lounge.

As Hamilton observes in her 2016 doctoral dissertation: "Very few pilots are identified by failures on random drug screens. Most information regarding a pilot's behaviors related to alcohol abuse or dependence comes from coworkers who may notice physical symptoms, a defensive or abrasive personality, or extensive rationalizations for unusual behavior. Other sources for identifying alcohol problems include disclosures made on flight physicals, FAA driving record screens, on-duty DOT tests, security screener reports, hotel incident reports, instructor and check airmen reports, family members and self-referrals." The message is clear. Be vigilant for airmen in need of treatment and rehabilitation.

Perhaps the Human Resource division of airlines should be more focused on creating constructive options for crew members stuck for a day or so at unfamiliar locales. For example, instead of time on their hands leading to default bar-hopping, line up a list of activities which would fit with the layover time required at a particular airport. Make such options easy for crew members to access and be proactive in educating them about the inherent risks of idleness in layover time that could lead to unhealthy activity like excess drinking. While it may be impossible and unrealistic to legislate how crew spend their off hours at layover points, I believe the employer has a responsibility to facilitate healthy options when that employer requires the employee to spend down time away from their home.

Furthermore, my research in this arena has revealed that some airlines' management (those above line pilots) still view the alcohol dependent pilot as having a character deficiency or moral failure rather than a disease demanding treatment. Others are simply unwilling to commit financially to the needed treatment expense for alcohol dependent pilot employees. Such roadblocks are truly unfortunate and suggest an absence of understanding among some management level leaders.

The HIMS online website (himsprogram.com) includes a menu subheading titled "get help now." Clicking on that opens choices including "pilot referral info." At the time of this writing there were 40 airlines with their contact information listed which I have reproduced at the end of appendix I.

A second important resource is the website for Birds of a Feather, the A.A. for airmen organization meetings, accessible at the link boaf.org. That website offers a subheading, "nests & contacts," listing towns/countries with "nests" as well as individual "solo" birds. Click the subheads for further details.

HIMS provides an extremely informative website which I encourage readers to visit and explore. Because residential treatment programs are foundational for starting the diseased pilot on his or her journey to recovery, I have borrowed verbatim the HIMS "recommended practices: treatment" section. HIMS does not establish certification criteria for pilot treatment, and hence there is no list of HIMS-approved treatment facilities.

Also, let me remind you that appendix I offers reproduced guidance/information directly from the HIMS website covering intervention, treatment, aftercare/monitoring, FAA recertification and pilot referral phone numbers and e-mail addresses.

Recommended Practices: Treatment

A. Overview

Treatment for the chemically dependent aviator is a critical decision in the recovery process. The HIMS program was based on the pattern of treatment and continuing care that has proved most effective in dealing with this illness, i.e. extended in-patient treatment and long-term continuing care. As the available treatment programs have evolved over the decades resulting in fewer facilities providing in-patient services and more providing residential programs, the HIMS model has been adapted to fit this reality. Today, extended residential treatment consisting of a minimum 28 days is the preferred modality. On occasion, with a diagnosis of mild to moderate condition, FAA has been willing to accept less comprehensive treatment modes. These modes, however, are determined on a case-by-case basis. For air carrier pilots, the need to ensure the safety of the traveling public generally results in a requirement for the pilot to participate in the 28-day minimum model.

HIMS does not establish certification criteria for pilot treatment. Consequently, there is no list of HIMS-approved treatment facilities. However, due to the nature of the professional aviator, and the unique requirements of FAA medical recertification, treatment facilities with a "professionals" program and experience in treating pilots are recommended. Additionally, HIMS and FAA's experience demonstrates that treatment at facilities with the following characteristics will usually result in better treatment outcomes and fewer delays in medical recertification.

1. a full-time certified physician addiction specialist on staff
2. credentialed and/or certified counselors, some of whom are in substantial recovery themselves
3. acceptance of addiction as a primary disease
4. insistence on total abstinence
5. separation of alcoholic/addict patients from primary psychiatric patients
6. psychiatry and psychology consultants
7. a strong family component
8. recovery program based on the 12 steps of Alcoholics Anonymous
9. endorsement by accreditation or licensure agencies

Addiction is a disease that affects all aspects of one who is afflicted: psychological, physiological, sociological, and spiritual. It is important, therefore, to find a treatment facility that addresses all these areas during treatment. Since treatment is the critical "first step" in a lifetime journey of recovery, it is essential to make that step solid and sure. It is not necessary to pay the highest price available to get this outcome, but one shouldn't settle for poor treatment that's provided at bargain basement prices. The quality of treatment is a far more important factor in selecting a treatment program than its cost.

B. Purpose

The purpose of treatment is multi-layered. All high-quality treatment programs will have a strong disease education component, personal and group therapy to identify personal issues and reconnect the patient with his/her anesthetized feelings, family therapy, support in developing lifetime recovery habits, and assist in creating relapse prevention strategies. Since chemical dependency directly affects all these areas, it is important to address each in order to provide a good foundation for further recovery. One of the most critical items that must be accomplished during treatment is breaking through the patient's denial.

Pilots are, generally, highly intelligent and skilled at compartmentalizing their emotions. These characteristics are very adaptive to their work environment, so it's not surprising that they are relatively common in this group. However, these same characteristics often reinforce denial behavior in this population. High intelligence allows for elaborate mental constructs that prevent the perception of alcohol or drug use as the primary cause for an afflicted person's difficulties. Emotional compartmentalization disconnects dysfunctional behavior from the emotional costs that would normally cause modification. Similarly, these characteristics and the special status afforded professional pilots often results in a sense of uniqueness that is counterproductive to relating to others. So, it is important for a treatment facility to be aware of these characteristics in order to effectively overcome the patient's denial defenses.

C. General Characteristics

As we previously mentioned, HIMS recommends treatment facilities that have a professional's program. Programs of this nature make it easier for the pilot to relate to other patients, which is an important part of breaking through his/her denial and creating a sense of "belonging" that will be essential to continued recovery. Programs that aren't professional in nature may reinforce a patient's sense of being different and therefore not subject to the same treatment requirements as others. Treatment facilities that provide a professional's program generally have well educated staff and provide a strong educational component to the treatment process. This environment is quite comfortable for a professional pilot, so it may result in a lower level of resistance to the treatment process.

However, when dealing with relapse cases, the patient has demonstrated an ability to "talk the talk" without being able to "walk the walk." The relapse is, therefore, a sign that a deeper, more permanent change is needed. In recovery circles it is often said that the longest 12 inches in the world is that which lies between one's head and one's heart. For the relapsed alcoholic or addict, that distance was not successfully traversed by the first treatment experience, so it may be beneficial for a second treatment to take a different approach. In this event, a cognitively oriented professional's program might not be as good a choice for relapse treatment as a more "down to earth" approach. There are very good treatment facilities that use each approach, but few that can effectively do both.

Finally, HIMS recommends facilities that allow for interaction between the patient and other recovering pilots in addition to his/her company representatives. In some areas, pilots in treatment are allowed to attend local "Birds of a Feather" recovery meetings. "Birds" is a group of recovering pilots who hold a meeting based on AA principles. Interaction with such a group can have dramatic positive effects on the patient's willingness to undergo therapeutic change. Additionally, early interaction with one's company supervisors can provide much needed security related to one's employment prospects and also helps establish a good "base line" for future interactions. Please consider this accessibility when selecting a pilot's treatment facility.

D. Location

One might presume that geographical location is a prime consideration for selecting a treatment facility. Our experience shows that it is not. While it is important that treatment include a family component, this type of therapy is usually conducted in the latter half of the treatment period. In most cases, the partner or other family members come to the facility for one or more days to participate in "family week." Since contact with others is limited to non-existent outside the treatment facility prior to "family week," being geographically separated has little consequence. Also, the access to travel benefits for a pilot and his/her family makes a multi-day stay at an out-of-town facility only slightly more inconvenient than what one would experience locally.

Sometimes a pilot in treatment will focus on family separation rather than his/her own situation. If the family is geographically close, this altered focus can be even more pronounced resulting in unneeded distraction from the treatment process. For all patients, damage has indeed been done to the family, and time and attention will need to be focused to repair it. But the time used for this purpose during the treatment process will be selected by the staff, not by the patient. In any event, repair of the family unit is a multi-year process and a patient's early efforts should focus more on one's self than on others.

E. Cost

As in any health care decision, cost of treatment is an important factor. A 28-day residential treatment program is, understandably, quite expensive. But research has shown that for every dollar spent on treatment and continuing care, companies receive $2-$11 in return. The return varies widely because of the different training and replacement costs associated with small and large air carriers. But all carriers receive substantial benefits in improved reliability and performance. For this reason, many carriers pay a substantially higher percentage of treatment costs than in some other areas of health care. Some carriers pay 100 % of treatment costs, and in these cases the company has removed any financial barrier to those seeking treatment.

In other situations, the pilot will bear a greater financial burden. Most health care plans will not normally cover 28 days of residential treatment, so certain pilot specific policies should be developed. Generally, a first treatment will receive the highest level of corporate financial support while subsequent treatment costs are borne more heavily by the pilot. Some corporations will provide no or low-cost loans while others permit non-flying duty following treatment to allow the pilot to earn a paycheck while awaiting medical recertification. There are also loans and grants available through many union organizations and some private foundations. On occasion, some treatment facilities have been willing to create payment arrangements for their pilot patients. But, regardless of the level of financial support, the cost of treatment is a bargain compared to the cost of an addiction. It is not unusual for a person to spend more in legal fees for one or more DUI's than one might spend on treatment. So, as someone in AA might say, "It's cheaper than drinking." And another adage that might apply is "You get what you pay for."

F. Company Involvement

HIMS encourages company supervisor involvement during the treatment process. A supervisor may attend mid-treatment "how goes it" meetings with the pilot and staff members. These meetings provide an opportunity to hear about the pilot's condition, personal issues, and treatment process directly from the treatment staff. Additionally, this meeting allows the supervisor to establish a supportive relationship with the pilot. The pilot will also understand someone cares about his/her situation and that their job is secure. So, many benefits can arise from this early interaction.

The supervisor may also attend an end of treatment meeting. This meeting will have many of the same benefits as the mid-treatment meeting, but it also provides an opportunity for signing a continued employment agreement. It's important the pilot understands and agrees to the conditions of his/her continued employment with the company, including continuous abstinence. Some companies choose to have this agreement in the form of a letter, but HIMS recommends an agreement written as a contract. A contract provides for a more explicit listing of the pilot's post-treatment requirements and its language is often more precise than the language used in a letter. And, while both documents have legal status, the contract form conveys this meaning to the patient more clearly than a letter. And, in many cases, the patient is asked to read the contract aloud before signing it to assure clear understanding by all parties.

Company involvement in treatment is not limited to treatment meetings and contract signings. In some cases, the company acts as a principal player in the choice of treatment facility. Since companies commonly pay for the majority of the treatment costs, it is not surprising they wish to make sure they receive a good return on their investment. In some cases, the company wishes to have its pilots treated close to their headquarters or a particular domicile to allow for easy supervisory involvement. So, before selecting a treatment facility, make sure the company's wishes are considered. Not doing so can result in unnecessary expense to the pilot or delays in getting recertified and returning to work.

Closing Comments

In recent years, science has shown that addiction to alcohol and/or a range of chemicals including nicotine is a stress-induced defect in the brain's ability to properly perceive pleasure. Stress changes the brain's ability to process dopamine which is the chemical associated with pleasure. A dopamine surge triggered by a drug causes the addict's midbrain to tag the drug as the new #1 coping mechanism for all incoming stressors.

Stress creates craving in the addict which leads to perpetuated drug use to satisfy that craving---temporarily. This present-day view of addiction holds that addicts are unable to resist the craving. Such unsatisfied cravings prompt externally visible behavior which is often unacceptable from both a legal and civilized societal view (i.e. crimes of all types and degrees).

Coping skills taught and embraced by Alcoholics Anonymous serve to relieve cravings and break the repetitive cycle of relapse to drugs and/or alcohol. While this author is a scientist by training, I will in no way seek to absolve the alcoholic from responsibility for his or her actions growing out of drug use. In my view we do indeed need to practice "tough love" in such cases. We must never confuse the labels of "victim" or "crime perpetrator." For those readers bothered by the preceding statement, you need to read my first book, *Triumph Born of Ashes: Trooper Mike Buckingham's Story*. In the book, the labels "victim" and "criminal" are shown and explained as starkly distinct and appropriate.

For those alcohol dependent pilots still in denial who want more hard data showing the measurable benefit of accepting HIMS-FAA alcoholism treatment and rehabilitation, take note of what follows. Heather Hamilton's 2016 doctoral thesis titled "Airline Pilots in Recovery from Alcoholism: A Quantitative Study of Cognitive Change" is convincing. The recovered pilot's IQ score measured by WAIS-IV at program entry and after five months of alcohol abstinence showed 12-14-point improvement for all age groups. Cognitive functioning broken down into index scores of verbal comprehension, working memory, perceptual reasoning and processing speed all improved by 8-11 % across all age groups. Archived data for the 95 pilots transiting the HIMS program 2009-2014 was used for her study with care taken to preserve anonymity of those 95 subjects. Although regaining licensing to return to flight duty was no doubt the prime motivator for these pilots, the prospect of improved mental health including improved cognitive functioning should help prod those in need of treatment to consent.

APPENDIX I: HIMS operational detail

This appendix content is taken directly from the very informative and well organized HIMS website (himsprogram.com). Website subheadings including "disease info", "additional info" and "get help now" provide the following detail. Be aware that the HIMS program and its relationship to the FAA continues to evolve, leading to changes which may not be up to date in this book by the time you read it.

HIMS Steps

It's Your Decision

The first step in getting help is recognizing there is a problem. Confidentially discussing your situation with a knowledgeable person is a great way to get started. This discussion will help you clearly define the issues and the available options.

There are several confidential resources available to assist you:

Use the Pilot Referral Info Section Pilot Referral Info section of this website to contact your company's HIMS representative.

ALPA members can also access information through the http://www.alpa.org website. Log in and refer to your airline's HIMS committee roster for contact information. Or, log in, click on "Committees," click on "HIMS" in the Pilot Assistance section, and click on the photo to send an email to HIMS.

Contact an expert aeromedical physician at Aviation Medicine Advisory Service (720) 857-6117, Monday-Friday 0830-1600 MT

Regardless of whom you contact, it's important to actively seek help for yourself or someone you care about

Assessments and Treatment

There are a number of substance abuse assessment and treatment options available. Generally, thorough multi-disciplinary assessments will give a better indication of the presence and progression of the disease. Which type of assessment is satisfactory for your circumstances will depend on several factors, including FAA or company involvement and available financial support. Your airline's HIMS/Pilot Assistance Committee or Employee Assistance Program resource will have the most current and complete information to assist you.

There are also a variety of treatment options available. Most companies have associations with particular treatment providers and using such providers can help limit insurance or financing problems. In general, these providers will offer a 28-day residential treatment program per FAA requirements. The FAA considers a minimum 28-day treatment program an essential qualification for the special issuance medical certificate.

Recovery and Monitoring

Following treatment each pilot will begin the process of FAA medical re-certification. How long this process takes varies considerably depending on each pilot's particular circumstances. However, a description of a "normal" minimum timeline is available under the "FAA recertification" prompt on this website's homepage.

If you have additional questions or require additional guidance, please contact HIMS via the link provided on this page.

Intervention

Background

Piloting an aircraft requires the highest levels of alertness and technical skill. Individuals who become successful airline pilots are generally intelligent and have strong ego structures. These characteristics are beneficial when operating an aircraft, but they can hinder the ability to break through a chemically dependent pilot's denial. Denial, of course, is a hallmark of the disease of addiction. It is explained in some detail in the Disease Model section of this website. Simply said, though, denial is the inability of the alcoholic or addict to make the connection between their alcohol or drug use and the negative consequences associated with That   use.

Due to the need for an uncompromising level of safety in aviation, it would be natural for someone to be concerned if they observed heavy or inappropriate use of alcohol or another drug by a pilot. We know that addiction, by its very nature, involves loss of control. And, the idea that a pilot with an active addiction is operating an aircraft is a scary one. We know, however, the presence of denial in an alcoholic or addict means they will often be unable to recognize they have a problem. A typical pilot's personality makes the task of getting them to see a different reality than their own a very tough assignment. An intervention is one method that has been shown to be effective in breaking through denial.

Definition

An intervention is an event that presents reality (specific information) in a receivable form (with concern) to a person unable to see that reality (in denial).

Goal

The goal of the intervention is to have the pilot in question agree to a professional substance abuse evaluation; it is not to try and get the subject to admit that they are chemically dependent. The diagnosis will be made, or not made, as a result of the evaluation following the intervention.

Types

Interventions are intended to interrupt the progression of chemical dependency disease. There are several types of intervention that can be conducted. The type that is used is largely dependent on the people involved in the intervention and the amount of information available. A useful way to examine the different types is to look at each as it relates to the participants involved. In all cases, it is imperative the intervention be led by someone who is trained in interventions. Usually, this means using a health care professional trained in substance abuse to lead, coordinate, and facilitate the event.

Classic

The "classic" intervention consists of family members and is conducted by an "interventionist," i.e. a trained therapist. Family members often have the greatest amount of information indicating a possible problem with chemical misuse. They are also emotionally significant to the person being intervened upon. Some of the difficulties with this type of intervention, however, are overcoming the existing family roles and dynamics. The family has probably enabled the pilot's drinking or using over time, and the pilot will use that fact as a rationalization to discount their current concern. Also, the pilot will have developed some strong defense mechanisms in relationship to any specific family member. It is also often difficult for the family members to provide credible negative consequences to the pilot in that they love him and are often financially dependent upon him. All of these obstacles and problems can be overcome, and, in many cases, a family intervention is the most effective of all types in breaking through an addicted pilot's denial. However, it should be clear that an intervention of this type needs professional assistance and that family members should not attempt to conduct an intervention without help.

Company Led

A company led intervention has both disadvantages and advantages when compared to a classic intervention. The company probably has less information specifically associated with alcohol or drug misuse. The company also has limitations on its authority to compel a pilot to undertake an assessment. These limitations may be statutory or contained in the company/union working agreement. The company may, however, be able to provide a highly significant negative consequence for the pilot's refusal to be evaluated: removal from flight status. The emotional significance of retaining his job is often a key in getting the pilot to agree to the assessment. However, one should realize that agreeing to the evaluation is not the same as breaking through the pilot's denial. A pilot may well agree to go to the assessment, and even participate in extended treatment, while maintaining internally that he "really doesn't have a problem." Of course, in this case, the long-term maintenance of denial creates a significant risk of relapse.

Peer

A third type of intervention is one that is led by the pilot's peers. This type of intervention is somewhat unique in that people who may be emotionally significant to the pilot lead it, but they are not in a position to provide a credible negative consequence. Peers may have much of the same information as the company, and sometimes more information, but the pilot will rarely agree to an assessment unless a credible negative consequence can be created. Most effective peer interventions are orchestrated to involve the company in some respect. They are often held in the Chief Pilot's offices without a company supervisor being present. The location allows the peers to present a circumstance to the pilot that demonstrates cooperation between the company and the peers. This setting causes the pilot to realize that lack of cooperation may result in further company actions.

Combination

The most effective intervention is probably one that includes all the people mentioned above: family members, company supervisors, and peers. However, such an intervention is extremely difficult and time consuming to coordinate and execute. This is not to say it shouldn't be done. If all the elements are present (a willing family, concerned supervisors, and willing peers) this type of intervention provides the pilot with the greatest opportunity for long-term recovery. But, delaying an intervention because one or more of these elements is missing can lead to a missed opportunity to disrupt the progression of the disease. "Striking while the iron is hot" is a phrase that can be well applied to interventions. The longer the time period that transpires between the precipitating event and the intervention, the stronger the pilot's rationalizations about the event and the more impenetrable his denial.

Do's and Don'ts

There are many things to do, and not do, when conducting an intervention. The most important thing to do is to control the event. Addicts and alcoholics are masters at deception and persuasion. From their perspective, an intervention threatens the very source of their comfort and wellbeing. They will take whatever steps are available to protect their freedom to imbibe in their drug of choice. A trained interventionist will take steps to control many aspects of the intervention. These aspects include choosing a location that is not comfortable for the pilot, maintaining tight control of the discussion to avoid arguments and cross-talking, and keeping the discussion factual and not blaming or criticizing. A properly prepared intervention will also include arranging for immediate transportation to an assessment/treatment facility and making sure the pilot has a bag packed. It is crucial for intervention data and workplace concerns to be transferred to the assessing professional.

There are dozens of other details to plan for and consider when conducting an intervention. It is not possible to cover every circumstance here, which is one of the reasons professional, experienced help is so critical. It should be clear, though, that an effective intervention may be a crucial step in getting a chemically dependent pilot the help they need. Without the intervention of loving, caring people, the future of the alcoholic or addict is very dim. The progression of this disease will often lead to incarceration, illness, or death. Over the past 40 years the HIMS program has played a critical role in preventing these negative outcomes for thousands of professional pilots and enabled them to safely continue the career they love.

Treatment

Treatment is implementing a systematic course of care. In the HIMS program, the term treatment is commonly used to refer to the specific residential or outpatient program given to the patient. But, more accurately, treatment is the sum total of all the efforts expended to effect a remedy for the chemical dependency problem. An ideal comprehensive program consists of the following elements: immediate intervention when warranted, rapid evaluation, assignment to the appropriate level of care, uninterrupted therapy, timely return to flying, thorough monitoring, and relapse prevention and contingency planning.

Design

The design of any treatment program must be congruent with the type of disease involved; that is, one must consider the particular characteristics of the disease and implement strategies to address them. Chemical Dependency has four characteristics. First, it is chronic, meaning it is permanent and prone to relapse. The disease for abnormal drinkers is called alcohol-ism, not alcohol-wasm! This description implies there is never a return to normal "social" drinking or any "recreational" drug use. Relapse means reactivation of the original disease, not acquisition of some new disease. To prevent relapse, one must implement a defense against the first drink or drug and build an ongoing maintenance program strong enough to countermand any alcohol craving or drug hunger.

Secondly, Chemical Dependency is primary, meaning it exists independently and is not secondary to some other underlying mental illness or personality disorder. Therefore, the addiction must be treated directly with measures distinctly different from the kinds of psychotherapy utilized for mental illness in general. These measures are not designed to empower one to return to social drinking or develop insight into why one drinks. Total abstinence from all addictive chemicals is the core goal central to this approach. If there is a co-existing mental illness, referred to as a "dual diagnosis" situation, then such illness is considered as another primary disease and treated accordingly.

Thirdly, addiction is predictable. It is most often progressive with four stages: early-middle-late-and too late! The consistency with which the disease manifests offers only three options to its victims: they wind up either locked up (incarcerated), covered up (buried), or they sober up (get into recovery).

Lastly, Chemical Dependency is catching. Its insanity is catching. The stress of living with an alcoholic/addict produces dysfunctional coping behavior similar to that seen in Post-Traumatic Stress Syndrome. Co-dependent family members often remark that they have lived through a "thousand Vietnams." Addiction is a family affliction, and therefore, any quality treatment program should have a strong family component.

Philosophy

The American Medical Association recognized alcohol dependence as a disease over 55 years ago. Aerospace Medicine, through the ALPA Aero-medical Advisor and the FAA Federal Air Surgeon, embraced this concept through the initiation of the HIMS program in 1974. At that time, the most successful programs began with extended in-patient treatment followed by long term aftercare extending over a period of years. HIMS adopted this treatment model and the majority of HIMS program participants attend in-patient or residential treatment for at least 28 days, followed by 3 years or more of weekly aftercare and monitoring.

There is no list of HIMS or FAA approved substance abuse treatment facilities. An initial diagnostic assessment should match the treatment to the severity of the disease, and health care professionals should consider the safety sensitive responsibilities of the professional aviator when recommending a specific level of care. With these considerations in mind, the HIMS program expects treatment programs to have certain components, including, but not limited to:

- A full-time certified Physician-Addictionist
- Credentialed and/or certified Counselors, some of whom are in substantial recovery themselves
- Acceptance of addiction as a primary disease
- Insistence on total abstinence
- Separation of alcoholic/addict patients from primary psychiatric patients

- Psychiatry & Psychology Consultants
- A strong family component
- Recovery based on the 12-Steps of Alcoholics Anonymous
- Endorsement by accreditation or licensure agencies

Approach

Therapy involves a tri-dimensional approach because body, mind, and soul are compromised. Detoxification and medical stabilization by the medical team occur first. Emotional balancing and cognitive restructuring follow and are accomplished by the counseling staff.

Finally, spiritual restoration begins with early exposure to Alcoholics and Narcotics Anonymous, which are mutual-help fellowships that embrace 12-Step programs. Initiating abstinence is merely the beginning of recovery, not the end. Making the changes in attitude, belief system, and habits necessary for the maintenance and growth of sobriety creates real struggles. The critical challenge is to make the transition from dry to sober, and from clean to serene!

Entry

Rarely does a pilot enter treatment completely voluntarily; most arrive because of some type of "benevolent persuasion!" Many believe their job is threatened. Fear of job loss often endangers their entire sense of being and identity. For most pilots losing their license and their ability to fly shakes the very foundation of their universe. Such circumstances often make the pilot suspicious and reluctant to fully participate in the treatment process. As goal-oriented people, pilots immediately set forth to complete the "check list," memorize the "manual," follow all "procedures," comply with all "rules," stay within the "envelope," pass the counselor's "check ride," and maintain the proper "glide path" to recovery. However, communicating on an intimate emotional level and becoming truly engaged in therapy takes an enormous effort.

Goals

Treatment involves accomplishing many goals:

1.Penetrating			denial
2.Understanding		the	disease
3.Reconnecting		anesthetized	feelings
4.Identifying	core	(personal)	issues
5.Involving		the	family
6.Developing	relapse	prevention	strategies

7.Inculcating Alcoholics/Narcotics Anonymous into daily living.

Modalities

When behavior is caused by disease, treating the disease changes the behavior! The old "28-day" residential treatment model is an endangered species. Today's state- of-the-art medical approach matches the intensity of the service to the severity of the illness. This approach applies to any disease. Not all diabetes is the same: there's mild, moderate, and severe, each requiring different treatment: diet, pills, or insulin replacement. The same is true for chemical dependency: outpatient, in- patient, or extended residential modalities are utilized. Pilots, like physicians, are often subjected to more strenuous approaches because of their safety-sensitive occupations. Nevertheless, individualized treatment planning is utilized to treat professional pilots.

Special Issues

Do pilots because of their common personality characteristics and unique working environment require specialized treatment? There has been speculation that pilots have "giant egos," that they are over-controlling, and are subjected to some very unique stresses. They often experience irregular and extended hours, intermittent "down-time," repetitive family disruption, altered physiology from time zone changes, sleep deprivation, and constantly operate with heightened vigilance waiting for some catastrophic disaster. The answer remains speculative. All recovering alcoholics and addicts are subject to stress, and the role of particular types of stress in reactivating addiction is unclear. The lack of consistent contact with supervisors and fellow employees does create some challenges to effectively monitoring pilots. But, such adaptations to specific circumstances also happen in other professions.

Myths

Two myths persist regarding treatment: 1) the alcoholic/addict must **want** treatment; and, 2) he or she must **hit bottom**! Both are untrue and can be circumvented by a process called intervention-- a compassionate, rehearsed, professionally facilitated, non-judgmental confrontation that essentially raises the bottom through benevolent persuasion.

Change

For a successful recovery from the disease of Chemical Dependency, the following must be changed: attitude, belief system, perceptions, thought patterns, and habits. Treatment is about motivating patients to make these changes. Therapy involves connecting the intellect with emotions. It necessitates abandoning isolation by establishing a sense of community. It requires acquisition of certain management skills, developing an accurate self-awareness, and above all, experiencing ego reduction at depth.

Success

Outcome studies show that the highest treatment success rates occur in the professional population, especially with commercial pilots. Rehabilitation, rather than termination, should be the ultimate goal, since it is much more cost effective to treat rather than replace a highly skilled pilot. Commercial airline pilots enjoy a significantly higher than average success rate, and in recovery, constitute a valuable asset to their profession and to the flying public.

References:

- Lewis, D.C. *A Disease Model of Addiction.* In *N. S. Miller and MC Doot (eds.) Principles of Addiction Medicine (1994). Chevy Chase, Maryland. American Society of Addiction Medicine, Section 1, Chapter 7, pages* 1-8
- Hankes, LR, and Bissell, L. In Lowinson, Ruiz, Millman, (eds.) *Substance Abuse, A Comprehensive Textbook. Baltimore, Maryland: Willams and Wilkins, 1992: 897-908.*

Aftercare/Monitoring
Overview

High quality aftercare and monitoring is the key to establishing long-term sobriety for the newly recovering pilot. Aftercare and monitoring consist of several elements, some mandated by the FAA and some not. The FAA Office of Aviation Medicine uses the term aftercare to mean the specific structured outpatient treatment that occurs after the initial intensive phase. This structured outpatient treatment usually includes periodic meetings with a psychiatrist and weekly group therapy sessions.

In a more general sense, aftercare and monitoring can refer not only to structured outpatient treatment, but also to meetings with peer monitors, meetings with company supervisors and employee assistance personnel, meetings in recovery groups like Alcoholics Anonymous (AA), contact with AA sponsors, relapse prevention visits to the pilot's treatment facility, and compliance testing. Most airlines with highly effective HIMS programs view aftercare for their pilots from this broader perspective and provide for pilot involvement in most, if not all, of these areas.

Recovery from chemical dependency is sometimes marked by relapse. Aftercare and monitoring are intended to address this issue. Of course, every relapse instance for an alcoholic or addict represents a direct threat to their health and wellbeing, as well as to the health of others. Additionally, a recovering pilot's relapse represents an operational risk to his company. These risks are often compounded because the pilot involved will usually not voluntarily admit to the re-use of the addictive substance out of shame, a desire to avoid re-treatment, and fear for his job. The shame and fear can then act as an incentive to drink or use again, and a vicious cycle may develop. The key to preventing such a cycle is, simply, to ensure it doesn't begin. The AA "Big Book," the main text for recovering AA members, says that continuous sobriety for an alcoholic requires a strong defense against the first drink. Effective aftercare and monitoring are the foundation of such a defense for chemically dependent pilots.

Sometimes people refer to the broader view of aftercare and monitoring as "continuing care." The use of this term, continuing care, is generally intended to indicate the need to address the potential for relapse: to, in essence, treat the patient against relapse. Since all the components of the recovery program act in concert, it is somewhat difficult to isolate one aspect or another as "treatment." Usually, however, the term "treatment" is reserved for the initial intensive phase of treatment (typically residential treatment for 28 days). Subsequent recovery program components are referred to as aftercare, aftercare and monitoring, or continuing care; and sometimes all three interchangeably. Because of their varying meanings, it is always a good idea to be specific about one's meaning when using these terms.

History

The understanding of aftercare and monitoring, and the view of the number and nature of the components that comprise it, has evolved over time. In the early years of the HIMS program, the initial success rate was good by contemporary standards, but not as good as was hoped. After reviewing the instances of relapse, the FAA added structured outpatient treatment with a therapist as a necessary requirement of the HIMS program. This change subsequently resulted in a reduction in the rate of relapse.

When the FAA examined the different varieties of the structured outpatient treatment experience, they quickly discovered that a group experience was by far the most successful. Individual aftercare sessions were not as effective as group sessions at preventing relapse occurrences. Also, less than weekly sessions were not as effective as those held weekly. Additionally, if the therapist was not well acquainted with addiction medicine, or if the therapist had a psychoanalytic perspective, the outcome was less favorable. Ultimately, the FAA determined the ideal picture of aftercare therapy should be a weekly group meeting of an hour and a half's duration. It should be a group of 8 to 10 recovering people and led by a health care professional familiar with addiction. The group dynamic should be both supportive and confrontational, with an emphasis on issues of life-adjustment as it relates to ongoing sobriety.

The FAA has found through experience with these groups that they are effective in the early identification of relapses. Also, however, the groups actually seem to prevent the occurrence of relapses. Fellow group therapy members, being in recovery themselves, are particularly sensitive to the signs of relapse. It is extremely difficult for a group member who is entertaining the idea of drinking or using not to telegraph that idea to other group members. It is an axiom of AA that a relapse occurs in the mind before it occurs in the body. It seems clear that relapse thinking is identified quickly in the group therapy context, and confrontation and support by group members can actually prevent the physical relapse. Importantly, in safety sensitive commercial aviation, one must maintain a non-punitive environment to encourage a recovering pilot's peers to openly voice any concerns they might have to program monitors. Such a non-punitive environment should not, however, preclude taking appropriate action should relapse behavior be unreported and ongoing.

Aftercare / Monitoring Periods

Aftercare and monitoring periods, as required by the FAA, have been extended over time. From the early days of the HIMS program which featured very limited or short monitoring periods, aftercare and monitoring in some cases today extends to the pilot's retirement age. As the previous discussion indicated, the group aftercare model is the preferred method of providing structured aftercare therapy. Typically, the FAA expects the group therapy to continue for at least two years after the pilot returns to duty. In some cases, it is beneficial to continue the group therapy beyond this initial two-year period. But the FAA also recognizes that, over time, studies show group therapy loses its effectiveness and that a pilot with a solid recovery will have less need of such treatment. Consequently, the FAA Office of Aviation Medicine has been responsive to initiatives from medical sponsors to reduce the level of group therapy involvement after the initial two-year period on a case-by-case basis.

The Aftercare Group Model

There has been some resistance to the exclusive use of the group model for pilots. Some of the resistance is associated with the difficulty of finding professional, long-term aftercare groups that are geographically convenient. Many aftercare groups are designed to provide a resource for the general treatment population and not for patients with professional licensing and regulatory issues. Some also focus on short-term support. Pilots in short-term oriented groups often become "assistant counselors" and stop benefiting from group participation. Some resistance has also been expressed about the frequency of the group meetings. Weekly meetings are difficult for pilots to attend due to the nature of their occupation. However, scheduling meetings less often than weekly has resulted in pilots making fewer sessions than desired.

As a general rule, pilots should be able to attend at least 50% of the scheduled weekly meetings in any significant period. This 50% level is considered to be the minimum frequency that will still result in the accrual of the maximum benefit for the participant.

Some airlines have group meetings at their domiciles. These meetings may include the participation of supervisors, union peer supporters, and members of the employee assistance program (EAP). Such meetings can be effective and useful in assisting the airman and in allowing effective communication and consultation among the various support team members. However, the FAA does not feel these meetings represent the specific aftercare experiences desired from the group therapy context. Therefore, even with the pilot's participation in such meetings, the FAA requires the additional presence of the preferred out-patient treatment group model.

Other Aftercare Components

As previously mentioned, in addition to FAA mandated aftercare, aftercare or continuing care can also include meetings with peer monitors, meetings with company supervisors and employee assistance personnel, meetings in recovery groups like Alcoholics Anonymous (AA), contact with AA sponsors, and relapse prevention visits to the pilot's treatment facility. Participation in any or all of these components may be at the discretion of the recovering pilot or may be mandated by the pilot's company. Usually the pilot's union, if present, will work in concert with the company to create a strong, effective aftercare program. Preventing a relapse by the recovering pilot is in the best interests of the pilot, the company, and the union's other members who may require HIMS assistance in the future.

Experience has indicated it is very beneficial to be clear and specific about a pilot's aftercare requirements. Some companies go so far as creating a specific, legal recovery contract with the pilot. Such contracts explicitly state the pilot's recovery requirements and the specific consequences for non-compliance with the contract's provisions. While the HIMS program does not make specific recommendations about the components of a company's additional aftercare requirements, experience has provided some knowledge of the effectiveness of how some components are executed.

Peer monitoring can be a critical asset in helping identify the early signs of a relapse. Peer monitors often are "graduates" of the HIMS program and have personal experience with the recovery process. Peer monitors are also viewed positively by the program participants, which helps them assist the pilot when he runs into difficulty. Peer meetings should, in our experience, be held at least monthly and face-to-face. Peer monitoring consisting only of telephone contact is seldom effective at identifying relapses or high-risk behavior that leads to relapse.

Meetings with company supervisors and EAP personnel, if held, should also be conducted monthly and face-to-face. Such meetings promote confidence in the pilot's recovery process and allow the pilot to develop a better relationship with his employer. Over time, these meetings help supervisors better understand the threats to a pilot's recovery and better manage the risks associated with other employees who may be suffering from chemical dependency disease.

Alcoholics Anonymous (AA), for many, is considered the cornerstone of long-term recovery for alcoholics. AA has spawned many similar organizations oriented toward specific addictions such as: Narcotics Anonymous (NA), Cocaine Anonymous (CA), Marijuana Anonymous (MA), etc. These groups often have associated support groups for those people in a relationship with the alcoholic or addict, such as Al-Anon. While many recovering pilots consider participation in these groups a core part of their recovery program, the groups are by design, anonymous. Such anonymity makes it very difficult to reliably ascertain the level of participation of any given member. None-the-less, some companies require participation in these, or similar, organizations.

Regular contact with AA sponsors has also been identified as very beneficial for pilots in the early stages of recovery. However, like AA, this relationship is one based on anonymity. Additionally, within the AA community, a sponsor relationship is afforded the same type of communication privileges as are publicly extended to doctor/patient and attorney/client relationships. But some companies still ask their HIMS participants to meet a certain frequency of contact with their recovery group sponsor, although the company has no knowledge of the nature of those communications.

Follow-up relapse prevention visits by the pilot to his treatment center are also sometimes encouraged. Such visits are usually limited to 2 – 3 days and rarely occur more often than once per year. Some pilots have reported such visits as helpful in strengthening their recovery program.

Finally, individual or family counseling is also sometimes recommended following initial treatment, or it may become warranted based on events later in the pilot's recovery. The removal of the addictive chemical from the pilot's life can have far reaching effects. In most cases, family dynamics will undergo major changes. The nature of the relationship with the pilot's spouse will be completely transformed or may end. The pilot may well experience the re-emergence of feelings that were long ago suppressed by the pilot's drug or alcohol use. In short, the changes to the pilot's personality and to other aspects of his life are both numerous and profound. The pilot's ability to cope with these changes can often be assisted by individual or marital counseling. But, in almost every case, neither the company nor the FAA gets directly involved in determining the nature or duration of this voluntary therapy. Of course, it is also the FAA's position that such individual therapy does not substitute for the group aftercare experience.

Monitoring

Monitoring, like the term aftercare, can have different meanings. Monitoring may mean the ongoing observation of the effectiveness of the various aftercare components. The term monitoring is also used to describe the abstinence testing conducted by the HIMS Independent Medical Sponsor (IMS) or the company.

In the context of monitoring as observation, the FAA sometimes speaks of monitoring the pilot's progress. When used in this way, the FAA is trying to express their need to observe progress in the pilot's recovery. Over the length of the monitoring period the pilot is expected to become comfortable with his sobriety and to avail himself of the available help when needed. Once his sobriety has become well established, the FAA may then reduce the pilot's aftercare requirements or release him from the special issuance program entirely. To assist them in their oversight of the individual pilot, the FAA desires as much specific information as practical. As a minimum, the FAA requires quarterly reports from the group therapist and prefers that those reports include a description of the therapy process, a discussion of the critical issues affecting he pilot's sobriety, and an immediate report of any adverse change in the pilot's behavior. Mere statements of attendance at the group are not adequate.

Monitoring can also refer to abstinence testing. All pilots diagnosed with the disease of chemical dependency or abuse must remain abstinent as a condition of their FAA medical certificate. Also, many companies require abstinence as a condition of the pilot's continued employment. Because of the nature of addictive disease, one cannot rely solely on the testimony of the recovering pilot. This is not to say that some pilots in early recovery aren't being truthful, it's just extremely difficult to determine who is telling the truth and who is not. Given this difficulty, it is imperative that an effective testing program be in place. Some HIMS programs leave testing to the individual IMS and, naturally, the testing is as random and thorough as the IMS makes it. In other programs, the company tests the pilot directly or employs a contractor to conduct the testing. Regardless of the method, however, a testing program has limited effectiveness if it doesn't include off-duty, random testing. Such testing should also be primarily oriented toward the recovering pilot's drug of choice but should include testing for other mood-altering substances. Finally, improvements in testing technology have provided an increased ability to "look back" over longer periods of time. If available, utilization of such tests discourages program participants from reusing while increasing the likelihood that those who relapse will be identified.

FAA Re-certification

The decision to submit the recovering pilot's case for FAA certification action is ultimately made by the medical sponsor. This sponsor is an AME (Aviation Medical Examiner) that has been through HIMS training and approved by the FAA to perform this duty. Often the medical director of the involved airline will perform this duty, other airlines rely on an independent AME.

The goal is to have the pilot in a stable recovery situation with treating professionals in agreement that he is ready for return to flight status. It is not beneficial to allow the case to proceed rapidly; often recovery will need the passage of time to be effective.

Time Line Chart

The time line chart below is helpful in understanding the various components of the FAA submission process.

It should be noted that the time for each step is an estimate. However, each step is an element that must be included in the package submitted to the FAA. We will consider them on an individual basis.

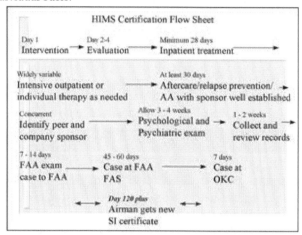

Evaluation

The FAA requires a formal 14CFR67 diagnosis with the multi-axial assessment documented. If the evaluation was done independently from the inpatient treatment facility, the complete history and rational for diagnosis must be included.

Inpatient Treatment

If the pilot was admitted directly to the treatment facility, this will be the source of the initial evaluation as reviewed above. If not, the treatment facility will also conduct an evaluation to confirm the diagnosis. This will normally be part of a history and physical examination that will conclude with diagnosis and treatment recommendations.

During the treatment program, individual and group notes are made on each patient. The evaluating psychologist and psychiatrist as well as the FAA will want these records as part of the submission. Also needed are the results of any psychological testing and personality issues. WE MUST INSIST THAT THE TREATMENT CENTER PROVIDE THE FULL RECORD, BOILER PLATE STATEMENTS ARE NOT ACCEPTABLE.

A discharge summary will be prepared when the pilot leaves the facility. This summary must recommend needed continuing treatment in the pilot's home area. This can range from intensive outpatient therapy (IOP), individual therapy, AA (always), aftercare group (always), and family counseling if needed. Many treatment centers take responsibility for identification of local continuing treatment resources. The best situation often occurs when the inpatient treatment facility is near the home of the pilot and continuing care can continue at the same facility.

Intensive Outpatient or Individual Therapy

This is often an extension of the inpatient program and must be continued until the pilot has made sufficient progress so that the weekly aftercare group is sufficient. Individual therapy may continue even after the pilot has returned to flight duties. In either case, after the pilot has progressed sufficiently to allow a recommendation for return to flight duties, a comprehensive summary is needed for FAA submission. This summary must give sufficient detail regarding treatment issues and progress made to allow the FAA to know where the pilot is in his recovery.

Aftercare and AA

The aftercare group is the cornerstone of sobriety after return to flight duties and will be mandated in the special issuance. The FAA submission must have a good summary of participation and progress. The group should be scheduled to meet weekly - the FAA expects the pilot to attend at least half to the meetings for the entire period of the special issuance. Failure to document the aftercare program in the FAA submission will result in delays in FAA certification.

AA, while not officially mandated by the FAA, is another cornerstone. The aftercare report should review the pilot's AA attendance and document that the pilot has a permanent sponsor. No documentation is required directly from AA.

Peer and Company Sponsors

Both need to be identified, to be trained and to understand how the meetings are to take place. The pilot is responsible for insuring that the monthly meetings take place and that the sponsor understands where the monthly reports are to go. The AME will need to document that sponsors are in place in the AME summary.

Psychological and Psychiatric Examinations (P&P)

The FAA has designated pairs of psychologists and psychiatrists around the country. This examination should not be scheduled until all of the above steps are in place and all agree that the pilot is ready for return to flight duty. A full copy of the above records should be sent to them prior to the evaluation. This is a very demanding and perceptive testing procedure. The pilot should not have the P&P if there is evidence of any residual cognitive dysfunction due to chronic alcohol abuse. More time should elapse to allow recovery. If the pilot is not in solid recovery, he will very often be identified as needing more treatment/time before flight duties. This in turn may require repeating the testing several months later.

FAA Examination and Submission

This is the final review before the case is submitted. The AME has full discretion to give hold the process until the pilot is thought to be in good recovery. The FAA package will contain the following information:

1. Diagnostic records (if separate from treatment)
2. Full inpatient treatment records
3. Summary from IOP or individual therapy
4. Summary from aftercare group with schedule
5. Full P&P report
6. Deferred 8500-8 (FAA Examination)
7. Summary from medical sponsor

The AME must carefully review all records to ensure that there is not a mention of an overlooked issue (e.g. One note deep in the alcohol treatment records mentions a use of cocaine that has not been addressed). The summary from the medical sponsor must have enough detail for the FAA to determine that the AME does indeed "know" the pilot and can legitimately endorse his return to flight status. The pilot must be otherwise qualified on the 8500-8.

The case should be sent to the Federal Air Surgeon's office via a package with a signed receipt.

Certification

The special issuance letter is very specific in its requirements. The pilot is responsible for seeing that each provision of the letter is met. The AME is authorized at any time to revoke the medical certificate. Return to flight duty is a particularly vulnerable time for the recovering pilot. A return to the same atmosphere that supported the addictive behavior is a time for heightened awareness.

Pilot Referral Information

(Author added: Be aware that the following individual airline contacts change frequently. The current contact listing is found at himsprogram.com under "get help now" opening "pilot referral info." List below is current as of January 2019)

1.ABX Air: Joe Riehl...Joeriehl63@gmail.com

(419)290-8962

2.AIR NEW ZEALAND: chairman Simon Nicholson
hims.simon@gmail.com

(642)174-7300

3.AIR TRANSPORT INTERNATIONAL: Ruben Vazquez
jetrube@gmail.com

(407)375-9396

4. AIR WISCONSIN

5. ALASKA AIRLINES: Bob Jones...bobo1778@gmail.com

(435)770-8689

6. ALLEGIANT AIR: Andrew Van Haecke...avanhaeke@yahoo.com

(406)439-9479

7. AMERICAN AIRLINES: Mike Galante...mgalante@alliedpilots.org

(239)821-8148

8. AMERIJET: Richard Carpenter...rcarpenter@amerijet.com

(954)608-8804

9. ATLAS AIRLINES: Regis G. Conti, Jr...bdlonghorn@aol.com

(954)554-8157

10. CAPE AIR: chairman Nick Massios...nmassios@gmail.com

(864)723-2961

vice chair Angela Inman...inmanak@gmail.com

                                                                    (561)603-0323
11.CATHAY PACIFIC AIRWAYS: Justin Peterson
                        justin.peterson@hkaoa.org
                        Ross Langley
                        ross.langley@aoagroup.org
12. COMMUTAIR: Nilofer Mallick...nilofer.mallick@alpa.org
                                                                    (914)475-7419
13. COMPASS AIRLINES

14. DELTA: chairman Warren Mowry...wmowry@bellsouth.net
                                                                    (678)357-7511
15. ENDEAVOR AIR: chairman Mike Lorenz...Mike.lorenz@alpa.org
                                                                    (913)568-2846
                        vice chair Chris Renk...chris.renk@alpa.org
                                                                    (440)292-7689
16. ENVOY: Owen Cotto...owen.cotto@alpa.org

                                                                    (786)343-8100
17.EXPRESS JET: chairman Troy Anderson.
                        Troy.Anderson@alpa.org
                                                                    (678)478-1765
                        vice chair Cater Davis...Cater.Davis@alpa.org
18.FED-EX: MEC HIMS chair Marc Grassie...marc.grassie@alpa.org
                                                                    (817)681-4757
19. FRONTIER: Tom Marks...tom.marks@alpa.org
                                                                    (303)916-0776
                        Darin Smith...Joejetdriver@hotmail.com
                                                                    (720)394-5583
20.HAWAIIAN: Thomas Henderson...Thomasehenderson@mac.com
                                                                    (808)341-3250
                        Pamela Huber...Pamela.Huber@alpa.org
                                                                    (808)224-6673
21. HORIZON AIR: chair Steve VanLandingham...
                        steve.vanlandingham@gmail.com
                                                                    (757)581-3158
22. JAZZ: Murray Munro...Murray.munro@alpa.org
                                                                    (403)616-3181
23. JET BLUE: Billy Petersen...william.petersen@alpa.org
                                                                    (516)818-8495
24. KALITTA: Dan DePiro...FLTtime@comcast.net
                                                                    (732)300-1012

25. MESA AIRLINES: Philip Colwell...philip.colwell@alpa.org

(803)984-8022

26. NETJETS: chairman Tim Markley...tdmarkley20@gmail.com

(614)578-1087

27. OMNI INTERNATIONAL AIR: Cole A. Lagrand

elocdnargal@yahoo.com

(480)747-3578

28. PIEDMONT: Roy Barker...rb1817@msn.com

(443)614-1537

29. PSA: Eric Cadarette...ecadarette@hotmail.com

(404)569-2212

30. REPUBLIC AIRLINE: Tyler Campbell...trawlscampbell@gmail.com

(859)992-7111

31. SKYWEST: chairman Jeff Mandrell...Skywest.HIMS@gmail.com

(618)315-0518

vice chair John Denando...SkywestHIMS@gmail.com

(314)283-3124

32. SOUTHERN AIR: Mark South...msouth@southernair.com

(515)778-8313

33. SOUTHWEST: chairman Tom Stanley...tstanley@swapa.org

(301)535-9871

34. SPIRIT: chairman Tim Helms...tim.helms@alpa.org

(954)684-6967

vice chair Jason Smith...Smitty4240@yahoo.com

(678)596-0763

35. SUN COUNTRY: Peter Piazza...prpiazza@comcast.net

(651)470-7263

36. TRANS STATES: Alan Musak...Alan.musak@alpa.org

(314)609-2406

37.UNITED AIRLINES: chair Margaret Hendrix

margaret.hendrix@alpa.org

(815)735-3491

vicechair Sean McKeown

sean.mckeown@alpa.org

(360)471-4426

38. UPS: chairman Brad Sayles...sayles.brad@yahoo.com

(865)300-6403

39. VIRGIN AMERICA: Charles Kinney...VAPA.kinney@gmail.com

(603)973-9045

40. WEST JET: chairman Ian Gracie...ian.gracie@alpa.org
(647)335-9735

APPENDIX II: drug facts

From the National Institute on Drug Abuse (NIDA) within our government's National Institutes of Health (NIH) comes a white paper dated August 2016 titled "Understanding Drug Use and Addiction." While not specific to alcohol, the findings are still relevant.

Drug addiction is a chronic disease characterized by drug seeking and use that is compulsive, or difficult to control, despite harmful consequences. Brain changes that occur over time with drug use challenge an addicted person's self-control and interfere with their ability to resist intense urges to take drugs. This is why drug addiction is also a relapsing disease...Most drugs affect the brain's reward circuit by flooding it with the chemical messenger dopamine. This overstimulation of the reward circuit causes the intensely pleasurable 'high' that leads people to take a drug again and again. Over time, the brain adjusts to the excess dopamine, which reduces the high that the person feels compared to the high they felt when first taking the drug---an effect known as tolerance. They might take more of the drug, trying to achieve the same dopamine high. No single factor can predict whether a person will become addicted to drugs. A combination of genetic, environmental, and developmental factors influences risk for addiction. The more risk factors a person has, the greater the chance that taking drugs can lead to addiction. Drug addiction is treatable and can be successfully managed. More good news is that drug use and addiction are preventable. Teachers, parents and health care providers have crucial roles in educating young people and preventing drug use and addiction.

APPENDIX III: chronic stress, drug use and vulnerability to addiction

From Yale University's Department of Psychiatry's director, Dr. Rajita Sinha, comes this provocative scientific article published in Ann N Y Acad Sci 2008 October. Figure 1 taken from Sinha's paper is reproduced below with associated article description.

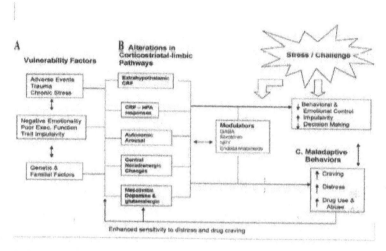

A schematic model of stress effects on addiction, representing the cross-sensitization of stress and drugs on behavioral and neurochemical responses, that are mediated by the stress and reward pathways. Column A lists three types of vulnerability factors: (1) developmental/individual-level factors such as frontal executive function development, negative emotionality, behavioral/self control, impulsivity or risk taking, and altered initial sensitivity to rewarding effects of drugs; (2) stress-related vulnerability factors such as early adverse life events, trauma and child maltreatment experiences, prolonged and chronic stress experiences; and (3) genetic influences and family history of psychopathology. Each of these factors influences each other to significantly affect alterations in neurobiological pathways involved in stress regulation and cognitive and behavioral control (Column B). Such changes at least partially mediate the mechanisms by which stress and individual and genetic factors in column A interact to increase risk of maladaptive behaviors represented in column C when an individual is faced with stress or challenge situations.

A more recent paper appears in Shanghai Archives of Psychiatry April 2014 titled "The dopamine system and alcohol dependence." Those authors conclude that "many of the currently available studies have contradictory results, presumably due to differences in methodology, non-linear dosage effects, use of different samples,

and the possible confounding effects of other neurotransmitter systems."
Nevertheless, science appears to be in broad agreement that there is a relationship
between the brain's dopaminergic system and drinking behavior both in animals and
humans.

APPENDIX IV: ALPA-HIMS evolving alcoholism policy statement

Sometime in the late 1970's (the document is undated but is located in the 1978 section of my father's files and quotes directly segments from the FAA November 10, 1976, white paper reproduced above), a document was created titled "HIMS SAMPLE OCCUPATIONAL ALCOHOLISM POLICY STATEMENT FOR PILOTS." The document was evidently a 'work in progress' because it is not identical to the final copy included within the final ALPA booklet published March 1982 and titled "An Employee Assistance Program for Professional Pilots (An Eight Year Review)." The booklet came with a cover letter dated August 27, 1982, signed by Dr. Masters (ALPA-HIMS Principle Investigator) and Captain Gilbert Chase (ALPA-HIMS Program Coordinator). What I have done is *italicized* parts that were removed or revised in the final copy and I have bracketed {**Bold-faced**} added and/or revised versions. One thing that comes through really strongly from viewing both versions is that those running this study learned that there was still a stigma associated with the word "alcoholism" or "alcoholic" ---hence, for example, the change to "employee assistance policy" instead of "occupational alcoholism policy" and "chemical" instead of "alcohol."

HIMS SAMPLE *OCCUPATIONAL ALCOHOLISM* {**EMPLOYEE ASSISTANCE**}
POLICY STATEMENT FOR PILOTS

Prologue

The most important reason for a joint ALPA/management *Occupational Alcoholism* {**Employee Assistance**} Program is that neither party can accomplish maximum results unilaterally. In any occupationally based program the objectives of both the union and management are identical because both want to assist the employee in recognition of his disease, restoration to full health and completion of a productive career to normal retirement. Such a joint effort maximizes the effectiveness of both the supervisor and the ALPA representative in properly assisting the alcohol-dependent pilot employee.

This Occupational Alcoholism Program is both preventive and remedial in nature. Its purpose is two-fold---first, it will focus on education with emphasis upon early recognition and self-diagnosis; second, it will make effective treatment available to ensure successful rehabilitation *and subsequent return to flight status whenever possible.* This program implements *authorized* company policy reflecting the active concern of _____ Airlines for its pilots who suffer from any phase of *alcohol dependency* {**any behavioral/medical problem**}. The policy is intended to provide a framework for the alcoholic employee to receive help, but success of this program can only be achieved through the cooperative efforts of ALPA and management to resolve in a rehabilitative and equitable manner the problems created by *an untreated alcoholic employee* {**misuse of chemicals and other behavioral/medical problems**}.

Objectives

The objectives of this *joint union* {**ALPA**}/management approach are (not prioritized):

1. To provide an atmosphere in which prevention, rehabilitation and aftercare can occur without pilot fear of job recriminations;

2. To establish a system of expeditious rehabilitation and medical case management with recommendations and {**professional**} assistance in voluntary disclosure of treatment to the FAA;

3. To provide the pilot with useable facts on the signs and symptoms of the disease which will include, but not be limited to, educational information in pilot recurrent training;

4. To appropriately identify *alcohol-dependent persons* {**those**} who require assistance, emphasizing self-identification techniques, peer group influence and the role of his {**ALPA representative and**} Flight Operations supervisor;

5. To jointly establish a referral system between the work place and an evaluation resource, which is professionally competent to diagnose the existence and degree of *the illness* {**a behavioral/medical disorder**};

6. To jointly support the treatment recommendations, if indicated, of the diagnostic/evaluation resource;

7. To {**periodically**} evaluate the effectiveness and efficiency of the program, thereby refining *the concept on this property* {**it as necessary**}.

Basic Points of Agreement

{**Most Employee Assistance Programs have a higher percentage of alcoholics than any other condition. Therefore,**} Our concern with alcohol dependency is directed toward the *employee's* {**pilot's**} performance on the job. As evidence of this concern, we have approved the following agreements which are preventive in nature.

1. _____ *Airlines considers* social drinking {**is**} the {**pilot's**} *employee's* independent personal   choice. However, the company recognizes alcohol dependency to be preventable and, therefore, encourages social drinkers to participate in available alcohol education programs.

2. The Federal Aviation Regulations define alcoholism as a "condition in which a person's intake of alcohol is great enough to damage his physical health or personal or social functioning or when alcohol has become a prerequisite to his normal functioning." This is recognized as the only operational definition applicable to pilots.

3. The company intends for this policy to be implemented in such a manner as to assure the *alcohol-dependent* pilot that his job security will not be jeopardized by his request for {**evaluation or**} treatment.

4. The company recognizes that *alcohol* {**chemical**} dependency is a *primary* treatable illness which can be *permanently* arrested with return of the employee to a *healthy* productive career. Pilots who may suspect that they have a developing *alcohol* dependency, even in its early stages, are encouraged to utilize the procedures which are available within this program and seek professional evaluation. Such self-identification and early assistance will benefit the *employee* {**pilot, his family, the**} company and the ALPA.

5. The company recognizes the confidential nature of the *alcohol* {**chemically**}-dependent employee's medical records and such confidentiality will be strictly preserved. However, it is recognized that, with the pilot's written consent, there may be a need to exchange necessary information between ALPA medical and _____ Airlines.

6. A pilot who suffers from this illness will receive employee benefits and insurance coverage the same as is provided for other illnesses under the negotiated group hospitalization and major medical coverages. Benefit coverage will also be extended to the pilot's eligible dependents.

7. *The company feels that* it is the responsibility of designated management and MEC personnel to cooperatively implement this policy and follow its outlined procedures. *Neither supervisors nor union representatives hold the medical qualifications necessary to diagnose alcoholism, thus necessitating referral to a resource jointly approved by* _____ *Airlines, the* _____ *Airline MEC, and the ALPA Aeromedical Office from which are available diagnostic and treatment recommendations* {**Supervisors and ALPA representatives hold neither the medical qualification nor responsibility to diagnose illnesses, thus necessitating referral to a jointly approved resource.**}

8. Because of the nature of *the illness* {**these illnesses**}, a pilot seldom seeks diagnosis and evaluation totally of his own volition. In such cases assistance from his fellow pilots and/or supervisor will be necessary. Any such intervention meeting must include both company and MEC- designated representatives. The decision to request diagnostic evaluation and accept the prescribed treatment is the personal decision of the individual pilot.

9. The company and MEC will make every reasonable effort to assist the pilot in making a decision to accept professional evaluation *and to follow the recommended form of treatment for alcohol dependency* {**from the resource jointly approved by company and ALPA Aeromedical**}. They will support the treatment and aftercare recommendations of the professional rehabilitation resource. If the employee refuses to accept evaluation and/or treatment, or continually fails to respond to treatment with indicators *of alcohol dependency* persisting in job performance, the resultant

company action will be consistent with any other situation which adversely affects job performance.

10. The company will periodically make available to designated flight supervisors and MEC representatives training seminars which will provide them with the level of expertise required to implement the joint company/MEC concerns expressed herein. *This training will assist these personnel in understanding the illness and how to assist the pilot employee in seeking evaluation and subsequent treatment.*

11. The pilot employee faces unique "return to work" procedures created by the FAA medical certification standards. Both the company and the ALPA will encourage the pilot to comply with federal disclosure regulations and jointly pledge their assistance during that process. *Pilots will receive applicable sick leave and medical benefits during this period and will be returned to work when found medically and legally qualified.* The final decision regarding disclosure of an excess drinking habit to the FAA is the pilot's, but failure to abide by federal regulations will preclude ALPA or company endorsement of return to flight status.

12. Pilots participating in this program will be expected to meet existing job performance standards and established work rules within the framework of existing federal, company and ALPA agreements. Nothing in this statement of policy is to be interpreted as constituting a waiver of management's prerogatives to maintain discipline or the right to take disciplinary procedures, within the framework of the collective bargaining agreement.

13. The MEC has designated and trained pilot representatives as the _____ Airlines MEC committee which will continue to work in this area. This committee will act in concert with their company counterparts to ensure that the full resources of both organizations are used to achieve the highest possible recovery rates. This policy has the full support of the MEC and the company, and it is intended that both will work together in the implementation phase of this program, in education and training programs, as well as in an ongoing evaluation of the program's effectiveness **{to assure continued improvement}**. *(author note: the order of items 10, 11, 12, & 13 were rearranged in final brochure as 13, 11, 10, 12)*

{HIMS SAMPLE LETTER TO PILOTS}

TO: All _____ Airlines Pilots **{and Their Families}**
Gentlemen:

_____ Airlines and the _____ Airlines MEC are establishing an *Occupational Alcoholism* **{Employee Assistance}** Program designed to assist pilot employees whose careers and health may be endangered by alcohol dependency {**or any other work**/. *We recognize that alcoholism is a primary illness which can be successfully treated and*, therefore, _____ Airlines and the _____ Airlines MEC {**we**} have developed a {**joint**} program which will make the services and resources of both organizations available to pilots who *suffer from this illness* {**may need assistance**}. This letter is to personally acquaint you with this new policy on alcoholism and our developing program.

The concept of *Occupational Alcoholism* {**Employee Assistance**} Programs has the support of the FAA as is reflected in a recent statement in which they support "efforts to identify and help those flight crew members who abuse alcohol...These may be individuals who, on their own, become aware of their ominously increasing dependence and addiction to alcohol and wish to do something about it, or those who are identified and persuaded that they may require appropriate treatment...The recovery rate among flight crew members should be greater than that of the population in general." *The Federal Air Surgeon is willing to consider petitions for exemption from the medical standards received from airline flight crew members.* {**The Federal Air Surgeon reports granting 77 exemptions for alcoholism industry-wide during 1976.**} These quotations illustrate the Federal Air Surgeon's current support for the goals and objectives of an approach which focuses on rehabilitation and FAA clearance for return to work. {**Furthermore, in 1976 the Federal Air Surgeon also announced that "marital counseling, family therapy, psychoanalysis, psychotherapy, etc. are not the basis for permanent, or for that matter, even temporary disqualification for FAA medical certification. Certain psychiatric conditions can lead to temporary or permanent disqualification, but these are of a severe order of magnitude, such as the psychoses and certain depressions which can result in definite prolonged impairment of the ability to function effectively. Beyond these serious states is a broad range of conditions and emotional and mental problems which can be successfully treated or alleviated by psychotherapy, and need not necessarily lead to disqualification by the FAA..."**}

_____ Airlines {**and** _____ **Airlines MEC**} has made a commitment to assist pilots during medical treatment and rehabilitation and any pilot who requests assistance for *alcohol* {**chemical**} dependency will not have his job security jeopardized by that request. CONFIDENTIALITY AND ASSISTANCE ARE ESSENTIAL INGREDIENTS TO THIS PROGRAM.

Pilots suffering from *alcohol* {**chemical**} dependency {**, as with any other illness,**} are assured of all the regular benefits {**as provided in your current Working Agreement.**} *including* health insurance coverage and sick leave benefits *while receiving treatment* {**will apply**} in an approved *medical* {**treatment and rehabilitation**} facility and until medically cleared for active flight status.

_____ Airlines and the _____ Airlines MEC have started this program to provide *alcoholism* education and assistance to *any pilot who needs* {**those who need or desire**} it. The enclosed policy statement forms the foundation for this occupationally based concept and additional information will be forthcoming. We earnestly solicit your full support for this *program* {**rehabilitative concept**}.

Sincerely,

MEC Chairman   Company Medical Director {**(If applicable)**} Vice President, Flight Operations

{HIMS SAMPLE OF PROCEDURES}

OCCUPATIONAL ALCOHOLISM {**EMPLOYEE ASSISTANCE**} PROGRAM---- BEGINNING IMPLEMENTATION PROCEDURES

Need for Procedures Specific to Pilots

The procedures for pilots must be distinct from other employee groups, thus accommodating the specific needs of the pilot's FAA medical certification process. Physical examinations constitute real or imagined threats to a pilot's continued medical certification and subsequent ability to maintain his livelihood. The airline pilot undergoes medical examination at least once a year and possibly as many as five times per year. No other industrial or professional group faces the total loss of their ability to maintain their livelihood and chosen profession due to loss of medical certification. In addition, airline pilots are professionals and, hence, render a service rather than producing goods. There is minimal direct management supervision which is complicated by variable hours of work and schedules of operation.

These factors and a number of others, when taken in the light of information gained from the available literature pertaining to *alcoholism* {**problem behavior**} in the occupational setting, have convinced us that the airline pilot's work environment is not well understood and does not fit the standard patterns routinely promoted by the National Council on Alcoholism and other astute observers on occupational programs. The unique setting of the airline pilot's professional career requires the input of persons who are very familiar with his job requirements, performance standards and medical certification. We, therefore, feel that special procedures for _____ Airlines pilots are indicated. These beginning procedural agreements are basic but flexible, thus allowing for adjustment and refinement to meet the specific needs of the _____ Airlines pilot group.

Procedures for Voluntary Referrals

For a few, self-awareness will result in early self-identification and a voluntary request for participation in the program. When such a natural intervention occurs, the pilot may go directly to his designated company or ALPA resource person or he may go directly to the approved professional diagnostic resource *(at the outset of this program it is agreed to be the ALPA Aeromedical Office in Denver)* {**jointly selected by**

Company and ALPA Aeromedical} to request evaluation and treatment recommendations. The pilot's voluntary request for help or participation in a treatment program will be held in the strictest of confidence (as are other medical conditions) and will not become part of his personnel file.

Other Procedures

In most cases, however, the pilot will be unable to recognize the extent of his problems thus necessitating an intervention involving appropriate individuals from within the company and pilot group. Intervention, as referred to in this program, is defined as "presenting reality in a receivable form" to a pilot who has evidenced questionable behavior inconsistent with his pilot profession. These concerned individuals will take appropriate steps to motivate the pilot to seek evaluation and follow the recommended course of treatment. Since denial and minimization are symptomatic of *alcohol* {**chemical}** dependency, intervention will be normative and should be jointly planned and carried out by designated ALPA and company personnel in accordance with the principles of intervention. They are:

1. Involvement of meaningful people;
2. Presentation of specific data associated with drinking;
3. Presenting it in an attitude of concern;
4. Offering the choice of *help* {**evaluation and following recommended treatment}** as an alternative to the consequences of problem behavior; and,
5. *Follow-up* {**Following through}** to assure completion of the intervention action.

An intervention focuses on the available data and selection of the offered choices, with neither company nor MEC appointees acting as professional diagnosticians or soliciting promises for total abstinence.

The planning, implementation and successful completion of such an intervention is a complex and sensitive task *quite different from the routine management of other behavioral/medical problems.* Therefore, a series of training seminars for select Flight Operations/ALPA MEC personnel will be required in order to fully orient the designated personnel with the strategies and techniques recommended to implement the intervention component of _____ Airlines Occupational Alcoholism Program. The ALPA Aeromedical Office has spent years developing a training curriculum which will be made available upon request to _____ Airlines personnel in a series of 1½ day workshops. The curriculum and staff will cover facts about alcohol, alcoholism, occupational programs, interventions, follow-up activities and FAA recertification procedures.

The company will select an appropriate Flight Manager (s) from each pilot domicile who will work in conjunction with the designated MEC and Medical Department personnel (_____Airlines and ALPA) and who will attend these seminars and share the responsibility for implementation of the procedures. Persons from this group will further develop and refine the preliminary procedures generally outlined in these comments and will establish and monitor a protocol for evaluation of the program's effectiveness and efficiency.

APPENDIX V: Doctors are human...so...why worry?

Dad's father by the same name, Ward Buckingham, had reason to embrace this appendix heading. Recall that his wife, Edith, died in 1929 of wrong side surgery when my Dad was only 11 years old. Dad had avoided sure death at least once in his airline career as shared earlier, and he had triumphed over the clutches of alcoholism that were taking him in the early 1960's to likely fatal complications. Recall too that he had tried to take his life twice during that downward spiral into what he described later as a "living hell on earth," and we three boys did not learn of that reality until receiving the letter in 2006 that Dad had sent his friend, Mike, in 1967.

I am the only member of this Buckingham clan going back several generations who chose to become a physician. I will reveal in advance that my 'expert witness' analysis was used by Dad's lawyer in successful malpractice action against the anesthesiologist responsible for the following travesty of medical care and its consequences. This is just one in a series of healthcare provider shortcomings to impact my close relatives and motivate me to speak and write in recent years about the critical need to enhance patient healthcare safety, advocacy and empowerment. Following is Dad's account provided for his legal team's use. I have omitted the offending anesthesiologist's name.

On or about 15 April 1982, when toweling after shower, I noticed a lump on left mid-chest. Lump felt as if attached to a rib and over some weeks appeared to be increasing in size and tenderness. I saw Dr. Schaller (author: Dad's internist) 1 June 1982 regarding lump and was referred to Dr. Martin 4 June 1982. Dr. Martin diagnosed exostosis left sternum and, after X-rays, suggested surgical removal of lump for biopsy. I agreed. Surgery was scheduled for 7 June at 11 AM at Highline Community Hospital. I checked into hospital 6 June for usual pre-op blood workup, etc. Early in morning 7 June I asked identity of anesthesiologist, and nurse said it would be Dr. ----_____ _____, 'a good guy'. I wanted to be sure he understood my feelings regarding the use of heroic measures to save a meaningless life in the event of an unforeseen accident during surgery. I had failed to make Dr. Martin aware of my feelings. Sedative medications were administered. Dr. _____ came in and discussed his anesthesia plan...pentothal and a nerve block of the affected area, and it sounded to me like a good plan. I vaguely recall being moved onto a wheeled bed and transported to a place immediately adjacent to surgery and Dr. _____ starting the injections. Before losing consciousness, I have the recollection of someone telling Dr. _____ to hurry up, that they were ready in surgery and that he was holding up the show. I next remember waking in the recovery room, moving toes and fingers on nurse's request...then being moved off the portable and into my bed. I recall my wife telling me the surgery went well and that the lump appeared benign. Shortly thereafter it became progressively more difficult to breathe, and I so advised my wife who summoned the nurse who attempted to administer oxygen by mask.

At this point the situation becomes somewhat clouded, but I remember becoming incontinent and had the impression of being an observer with no further sensation except hearing. Conversations reporting erratic blood pressure readings, much scurrying and a feeling of being moved from bed to bed, always with the infernal suffocating mask. I seem to recall a voice (I think, Dr. Schaller) saying 'you're losing him'. I remember gagging and vomiting when intubation attempts were made. A newcomer arrived and I recall that he soon had the situation under control. I remember an eyelid being raised and a light flashed in my eye, an X-ray plate being placed under me, tubes and pumps being ordered, and the term 'bilateral pneumothorax' being used. I regained full consciousness to find two nurses peering at me and found myself unable to talk because of the breathing device. By signing to the nurses, I was provided a pencil and paper so that I could communicate. The most unpleasant feature of the entire fiasco was not pain or the probability of death, but the likelihood of survival with grossly impaired mental capability, and that I had forgotten to tell the medical staff of my feelings regarding 'heroic measures'.

I'm told that what happened to me 'is not unusual'. However, one lung is generally involved, and the collapse occurs during surgery. From a layman's position, it appears a mistake was made by the anesthesiologist, that fact was not communicated to any personnel involved, the emergency room doctor was incapable of diagnosing what had happened and did not at once seek help from a lung-thorax specialist, and a portable chest X-ray ordered by Dr. ... . at 14:10 was not accomplished until 15:10.

Changes noted since incident:

1. Difficulty with abstract thought processes and improvising.

2. Tendency to become addled when faced with unfamiliar set of circumstances.
3. Difficulty in decision making.
4. Eye, thought, muscle coordination impaired.
5. Increased discomfort and numbness left arm, hand & fingers. Some discomfort and numbness were present before following cervical laminectomy in 1975 but has increased markedly since 7 June 1982 and is now noticeable in right arm and hand.
6. Necessary to get up at night to relieve bladder, disrupts sleep.
7. General feeling of malaise.

He then listed my name and contact information, and he specified that I would not talk with other than his primary lawyer without him otherwise specifying. I was 400 miles away when this event happened. However, I obtained a copy of the hospital chart and readily volunteered to serve Dad's lawyer as "expert witness" by reviewing the record and providing my written assessment. This was, indeed, an egregious example of medical malpractice. Before recording my assessment, I'll add a separate correspondence with his lawyer dated April 20, 1983, wherein Dad reported the following changes noted in physical and mental conditions since that June 7 misadventure:

1. Much lower exercise tolerance---shortness of breath.
2. Periods of near passing out during mild exercise. These seem to be alleviated with a medication tenormin 50 mg. This medication has been used since early February as a result of ventricular arrhythmia diagnosed after 24-hour surveillance by Holter monitor.
3. Persistent hoarseness of voice and periods of inability to speak intelligibly caused by vocal cord trauma during intubation.
4. Disrupted sleep pattern due to necessity of getting up at night to relieve bladder.
5. Eye, thought, muscle coordination markedly deteriorated. Previous fine muscle control no longer present.
6. Persistent metallic odor to urine which indicates to me that body chemistry is drastically changed due to incident.
7. I have always been regarded as mentally and physically young for my chronological age. Since 7 June 1982, incident, it is apparent the reverse is true.

On October 20, 1982, four months after this travesty of medical care, I submitted a five-page detailed analysis of Dad's medical care and hospital chart regarding this incident. I also took the initiative to call and speak with the chairman of the

Washington State Medical Association professional liability review committee. While errors leading to bad results can and do occur as we human beings probe our patients, and such errors do not necessarily violate the standard of practice, errors especially of omission were egregious here. There was no record of a PAR conference between Dad and the anesthesiologist pre-operatively. While the anesthesiologist knew he had aspirated air on one side as he was doing his rib blocks, he made no chart entry of same, he made no request for a post-op chest X-ray to evaluate for pneumothorax, and he wrote no order for nursing staff to observe for possible pneumothorax post-op. Meanwhile, the hospital committed egregious error by taking one full hour to obtain a portable chest X-ray where the written order read "portable chest X-ray now" and the patient was then cyanotic complaining of inability to breathe. As a result of delay in diagnosis, Dad suffered sequelae of hoarseness from urgent traumatic intubation of his airway and the experience of being tied for hours to a respirator. This case dragged on over nearly 3 years before Dad was awarded damages, but that monetary award did not undo the changes he listed that he was left to live with. For those readers savvy with medical science, Dad's arterial blood gas values drawn when he was seizing, incontinent, cyanotic, and showing interventricular conduction defect on EKG were reported back 10 minutes before the chest X-ray finally got done...pH 6.86 and pCO_2 122...do you suppose those results had anything to do with chest X-ray ordered 50 minutes earlier now getting done pronto? Yet Dad's lawyer did not want to include the hospital in the suit action, justifying same by saying "we have had some good results with the adjustor who is handling this matter on behalf of the physician's insurance company" and "the adjustor for the hospital would probably convince the adjustor for the doctor that her evaluation of the case is too high." Let me just conclude this by saying that the hospital is extremely fortunate that Dad survived this extreme stress test.

Seven years later, some of our family (including me) felt that Dad was harboring bitterness and/or resentment over the lingering side effects of that incompetent anesthesiologist's care. **I thought it wise to write him about this apparent unforgiving spirit, and I share part of his response to me in hopes that other readers can profit from my mistake. It is folly to presume one knows the true heart of another and render judgment as I did in this instance:**

Dear Ward,

I'm not exactly unfamiliar with the deleterious effects of harboring resentments. I suspect my feelings toward the incompetent you mentioned are similar to yours toward the legal profession. It's too bad you don't find my spiritual condition to your liking---that's not my problem. Acceptance seems to be yours. The fact that I have not embraced the program with the fervor that you demonstrate does not, in my mind, make me a lesser Christian than you. A man's relationship with his God is a very personal relationship. I appreciate your concern for my spiritual and physical health, but I assure you that I will not give up the spiritual program that gave me back my life almost 24 years ago in order to participate in one you feel is better.

Love, Dad

This is an opportune time to present information which was key to Dad's embrace of lasting sobriety, and it is found clearly expressed in the book, "Alcoholics Anonymous." The first edition was published in 1939, and I am drawing from the revised 1955 edition which preserved largely intact the details of the A.A. recovery program. Realize that A.A. membership was scarcely 100 when that original version appeared, and that first edition represents a consensus composition without single named authorship. Without discounting the import of the remainder of this 565-page treatise, I will quote the only portion of my parents' copy that was underlined by them:

We are going to know a new freedom and a new happiness. We will not regret the past nor wish to shut the door on it. We will comprehend the word serenity and we will know peace. No matter how far down the scale we have gone, we will see how our experience can benefit others. That feeling of uselessness and self-pity will disappear. We will lose interest in selfish things and gain interest in our fellows. Self-seeking will slip away. Our whole attitude and outlook upon life will change. Fear of people and of economic insecurity will leave us. We will intuitively know how to handle situations which used to baffle us.

A.A. makes clear that "faith alone is insufficient" in one's quest for the lasting sobriety of recovery from alcoholism. "To be vital, faith must be accompanied by self-sacrifice and unselfish constructive action." Recall my earlier citing of the import to Dad of that 12th step of A.A. which reads: "Having had a spiritual awakening as the result of these Steps, we tried to carry this message to alcoholics, and to practice these principles in all our affairs." That action step was paramount in his remaining 28 years of sobriety as he reached out to others trapped in alcoholic bondage he himself had known so well. While I am confident my father was neither an agnostic nor atheist, his externally visible life did not include church attendance or Bible reading. However, I had no business criticizing his practice of faith. As the A.A. book states, "The main thing is that he be willing to believe in a Power greater than himself, and that he live by spiritual principles."

One of numerous Chesterfield cigarette ads of the 1950's and 1960's in which Dad appeared as he does above. As noted in following pages, he died of lung cancer.

APPENDIX VI: reflections

Dad died Christmas eve 1994 just short of his seventy-seventh birthday. Although he quit smoking 8 years before death, lung cancer took him which is in keeping with the reality of residual heightened lung cancer risk for those who don't quit smoking before age 50. Ironically, his handsome face often graced cigarette ads, especially in the 1950's before published evidence of smoking's dangers to health became prevalent. One former Pan Am employee recalls even seeing him pictured in a poster for Buckingham cigarettes, a brand that none of the family recall him using himself. The Chesterfield ad pictured here came from a New York theater program in 1959, early in the commercial jet age. What follows is what I shared at his memorial service which drew airmen from far and wide:

Dad,

I guess you know we have never had what others might term a really close father-son relationship. Yet we both know we both loved and respected one another. Some of my earliest memories are of fishing trips together in Montana...what a legacy your father left us all at Bitterroot Lake's "Buckingham Palace!" You modeled the importance of respect for our older family relatives by spending many summer vacations there with numerous of your relatives. We fished, swam, water-skied, played cribbage, hiked and listened to Grandpa Ward tell stories of turn-of-the-century life with Indians in eastern Montana. We spent many Christmas and Spring vacations as a family skiing The Big Mountain in Whitefish.

As you were increasingly gripped by your alcoholism you continued to encourage me toward a career in medicine, even at times suggesting to me you wished you had been a physician. I saw what real commitment to one another requires as Mother stood by you through the darkest point in your life in the mid-1960's until you achieved permanent sobriety in 1966. It was that year that I accepted Christ, realizing that I was powerless to solve your alcoholism. I saw you approach life with a new vigor and awareness after you achieved sobriety. You seemed to become ever more aware of and concerned about the needs of others around you. I saw you take leadership roles in helping fellow aviators achieve sobriety. When mandated retirement at age 60 arrived in 1978, you chose to press on in your second career of helping others rather than take life easy. You went back to school to obtain another college degree, this in alcoholism counseling. I saw you give back to those who had helped you in your time of need.

In spite of all your involvements the past 20 years or so outside the home helping others, you always made an effort to encourage me and my family in so many ways. Remember your idea of gathering we three boys, with our wives and children together with you and Mother for a family ski vacation at Jackson Hole in the late 1970's, the last time your chronic neck pain permitted you to ski. Remember the three summer horse pack trips 1978-1980 to the Bob Marshall Wilderness you organized and invited we three boys...what special man times together! Thanks for the numerous times you helped financially from the loan for our first home down payment in 1975 to the numerous outright financial gifts. Thanks for the encouraging words you've given us repeatedly about our daughters, Erika and Julie, and the many positive affirmations you've given each of them. You taught me the importance of living life conservatively even though your finances would have allowed you to lavish fancy cars and outward markers of material wealth on yourself. You taught me the importance of giving financially to others.

When your cancer was diagnosed on your birthday in 1993, I knew the disease was fatal barring some miracle. Yet you battled on against the odds and endured some real tough times in the process. Remember the night we three boys spent with you at the hospital about a month after diagnosis when you shared your heart on many matters with us as you lay critically ill with sepsis, pneumonia and chemotherapy-induced bone marrow suppression. You even shared light moments in your past then like the time Elizabeth Taylor sat on your lap in the 747 cockpit as you arrived at the Los Angeles terminal! Two months ago, when you learned the cancer had spread to your brain, you no longer wanted to play cribbage. Even though your superior intellect did not seem damaged to me, you were aware that it was not up to your high standard and did not wish to play mind games like cribbage anymore. I admired you all the more then because pride does have positive value even though we males have been justifiably criticized in the past for being too prideful. You have always been interesting to talk with, well read on almost any subject, a testimony to your interest in the world around you and your voracious reading habits.

It was very difficult for me to be down in Coos Bay the last two weeks, busier than at any time in my twenty years there, knowing that you were dying and I was not there. When I did arrive for our last earthly visit, I'm not surprised you greeted me out of delirium with "what took you so long?" A few hours earlier you had maintained your customary stoic attitude for your doctor when he made a home visit and you denied being in any pain. But we realize you wanted all the family (Mother and we three boys) there one last time before you gave up your struggle. And we had the opportunity to share with you then that it was just fine to "let go and let God", that He would take you to be with Him where there would be no more pain and suffering, and that we three boys and Mother would all be reunited with you someday to enjoy life eternal in Heaven as Christ promised to all who place their trust in Him. Three and one-half hours after I left your bedside Christmas eve you physically died. We miss you but we are relieved you are no longer suffering. And thank you for making a miraculous appearance to Mother as your spirit headed Heaven-wards. It is as if you and our Lord knew Mother would harbor guilt at not being at your bedside as you took your last earthly breath. So, as she was down the hallway in the kitchen at that moment, you appeared distinctly to her in a flash dressed in your raincoat appearing your handsome self, looking directly at her that instant. We love you and always will. And I just want you to know I've still got that handwritten letter from Grandpa Ward to me, written in 1952 when he was 77 years old (the same age as you at your death), where he advised me to "never forget that a boy's best friends are his father and mother."

The last item entered by Dad in his 3-ring binder previously alluded to is his curriculum vitae recorded in 1981 and reproduced below:
<u>EDUCATION:</u>
   *Bachelor of Arts degree in engineering, University of Montana, 1941
   *Certificate Program in Alcohol Studies, Seattle University, 1978
   *Completion Human Intervention and Motivation Studies, Air Line Pilot
      Association Seminars, 1975
     *Tutelage in the field of alcoholism under Dr.Joseph A. Pursch,
        Capt. USN and Director of Navy Alcohol Recovery Program;
        Vernon Johnson, Johnson Institute Founder; Ross A.
        VonWiegand, Director of Labor Management Services, NCA

(National Council on Alcoholism)
*Physician Training Program on Alcoholism, Care Manor
   Hospital, Orange CA
EXPERIENCE:
*Thirty-six years Air Transportation (Pan Am) as pilot in
   command; management functions as Chief Pilot, Flight Manager;
   ALPA Union functions as Council Chairman; Chairman, Master
   Executive Council Professional Standards & Aero Medical
   Committee, ALPA
* Advisor to Human Intervention and Motivation Study, Airline
   Pilots Association, 1973-1978
*Assistance to United Air Lines (UAL), Pan Am, and other air
   carriers in establishment of alcoholism programs
*15 years counseling flight crew members with alcoholism
*Since 1975 personal association with Federal Air Surgeon & staff
   regarding licensing problems and procedures with airmen having
   alcoholism
*Participation in NCA "Operation Understanding No. Two", San
   Diego CA., 1977 (NCA refers to National Council on Alcoholism which
   in 1990 became NCADD, National Council on Alcoholism and Drug
   Dependence...author added)
*Holder of FAA exemption for alcoholism number M-10590, June
   17, 1977
*Certificated Alcoholism Counselor
*Industrial Consultant, Southwest Community Alcohol Center

I need to add that throughout much of the 1980's and early 1990's Dad
volunteered regularly for Seattle's Helpline for addiction.

Retired Airman
Capt. Ward Buckingham
1918-1994
Co-Founder "Birds" B.O.A.F.

BIBLIOGRAPHY

1. "Alcohol and The Airline Airman", term paper for college class 1978 (Survey on Alcoholism)

2. "Reflections on Complexity", term paper for college class 1978 (Personal and Social Rehabilitation of the Alcoholic)

3. HIMS Sample Occupational Alcoholism Policy Statement for Pilots

4. Address to Alcohol Awareness Hour, Eisenhower Medical Center, 1978

5 Pakull, Barton. "Alcoholism and Aviation Medical Certification". Alcoholism: Clinical and Experimental Research, Vo.2, No.1, 1978

6. Federal Aviation Administration. Exemption No. M-10590

7. Federal Aviation Administration. Alcoholism and Airline Flight Crewmembers. Nov. 10, 1976.

8. Modell, Jack G. and Mountz, James M. Drinking and Flying---The Problem of Alcohol Use by Pilots. N Engl J Med 1990; 323: 455-461.

9. Federal Aviation Administration. Guide for Aviation Medical Examiners. 2017

10. The HIMS Handbook. Revised August 2014

11. Hui, M A and Gang, Zhu. The Dopamine System and Alcohol Dependence. Shanghai Arc h Psychiatry. 2014 April; 26(2): 61-68

12. Sinha, Rajita. Chronic Stress, Drug Use, and Vulnerability to Addiction. Ann N Y Acad Sci. 2008 Oct; 1141: 105-130

13. Birds of a Feather (BOAF). Access website at www.boaf.org

14. Human Intervention Motivation Study (HIMS). Access website at www.himsprogram.com

15. Hamilton, Heather C. Airline Pilots in Recovery from Alcoholism: A Quantitative Study of Cognitive Change. 2016 doctoral dissertation.

16. Masters et al. An Employee Assistance Program for Professional Pilots (An Eight Year Review). Human Intervention Motivation Study. March, 1982.

17. Wegscheider, Sharon. Another Chance: Hope and Health for the Alcoholic Family. 1981.

18. Gordon, Suzanne et al. Beyond The Checklist. 2013.

19. Prouse, Lyle. Final Approach. 2011.

Plus numerous letters; memorandums; 'white papers' from, to and amongst airlines, ALPA, FAA and their employees. Also, phone calls and e-mails between me and numerous sources.

Made in the USA
Middletown, DE
11 March 2022